Jonathan Meades is a writer, journalist, es
of *Filthy English, Peter Knows What Dick I*
The Fowler Family Business, Museum With
Pedro and Ricky Come Again. From 1986–2001 ʰᵉ ᵂⁱ⁻⁻⁻
mately about restaurants in *The Times*.

He has written and performed in many television films, among them *Jerry Building, Joe Building, Ben Building, Magnetic North, Off Kilter, The Joy of Essex, Father To The Man* and *Meades Eats*, a three-part series about what the English really consume.

Unbound published *Pidgin Snaps*, a boxette of a hundred of his photos in post-card form. In the spring of 2016 his exhibition *Ape Forgets Medication* comprised thirty artknacks and treyfs. *The Plagiarist in the Kitchen* is the only cookbook he will ever write.

JONATHAN MEADES

The Plagiarist in the Kitchen

unbound

First published in 2017
This paperback edition first published in 2021

Unbound
Level 1, Devonshire House, One Mayfair Place, London, United Kingdom, W1J 8AJ

www.unbound.com

Text design by Patty Rennie

A CIP record for this book is available from the British Library

ISBN 978-1-78352-852-3 (trade pbk)
ISBN 978-1-78352-240-8 (trade hbk)
ISBN 978-1-78352-241-5 (ebook)
ISBN 978-1-78352-303-0 (limited edition)

Printed in Great Britain by CPI Group (UK)

1 2 3 4 5 6 7 8 9

For Angelica and Laurie

Contents

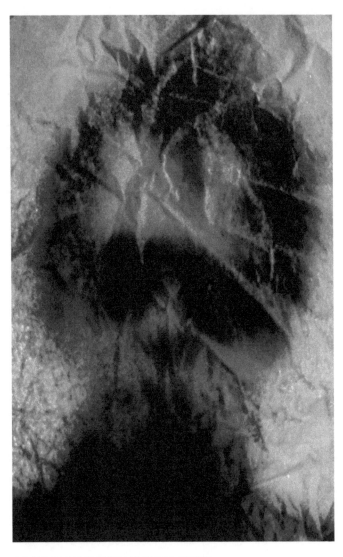

ALL SNAPS IN THIS BOOK ARE BY THE AUTHOR

The Plagiarist in the Kitchen is an anti-cookbook, a recipe book that is also an explicit paean to the avoidance of culinary originality (should such a thing exist), to the daylight robbery of recipes, to hijacking techniques and methods, to the notion that in the kitchen there is nothing new and nor can there be anything new. It's all theft. Anyone who claims to have 'invented' a dish is dishonest or delusional or foaming. The very title was lifted, without permission and with the gracelessness that infects Cooking World, from Julian Barnes' *The Pedant in the Kitchen* (plenty more to rip off there). Informed of this larcenous book's imminence Barnes prudently and no doubt correctly elected to consider it an act of homage.

Letting on where the title came from and fessing up to the book's dogged thievery promotes a collision.

Were it a work of genuine plagiarism I would not have admitted it. I'd have covered my tracks – unlike the thief who returns to the scene of the crime. I'd have called it something different and altered recipes, using, for instance, mackerel instead of crème anglaise and substituting glacé fruits for sweetbreads.

Were it a work of genuine plagiarism I would, in an access of bovarysme, have convinced myself it was original. All that's original are my monochrome treyfs.

Apart from myself the most frequent victim of my light fingers is the greatest of all cooks, Anon.

BASIC

STOCK

A restaurant might have as many as 5 or 6 stocks on the go. There's seldom the room, seldom the need in a domestic kitchen. One will suffice. Avoid stock cubes and supermarket stocks. I rarely include wine and don't use lamb or pork (the latter's feet apart).

Any combination of:

LEFTOVERS AND BONES AND CARCASSES OF

BEEF

VEAL

CHICKEN

DUCK

GUINEA FOWL

PHEASANT

PIG'S TROTTER

CALF'S FOOT

ONION

GARLIC

CARROT

CELERY

FENNEL

LEEKS

DRIED TOMATO

DRIED CEP

DRIED ORANGE PEEL

JUNIPER BERRIES

MUSTARD SEEDS

PEPPERCORNS

BAY LEAVES

WATER

(WINE, DRY, WHITE)

ROASTING JUICES IF YOU'RE STARTING WITH A LEFTOVER
DUCK OR BEEF RIB. NEVER WASTE ANYTHING.

Bones, carcasses, feet and vegetables are best browned in a hot oven to enrich the ultimate flavour – don't overdo it, don't let them catch. Deglaze their vessel with water. However, there's not much to be gained by browning scraps of already cooked meat. The greater the quantity of meat and bones, the more gelatinous, smoother and deeply flavoured the stock will be.

Use a large pan – 10 litres or so. Cover the meat and veg and spices with cold water (and dry white wine). Bring to near a boil, but don't allow the stock to do anything other than just simmer. If it boils the ingredients will break down and it'll get cloudy. Skim the top every now and then to rid it of the grey murk. Leave to cook for about eight hours.

Strain through a sieve with a double layer of muslin. Strain again.

It can now be boiled and reduced to whatever density is required.

Refrigerate. It'll turn to jelly.

'SEASON ... SALT ... MAYBE PEPPER (CAN BE WHITE) ... REMOVE THE GERM FROM GARLIC ... COOK SPICES ... BOIL OFF ALCOHOL ... COOK TO PLEASE YOURSELF AS YOU MIGHT WRITE OR PAINT, DANCE OR SING TO PLEASE YOURSELF ... CREATE YOUR OWN THEFTS ...

It ought not to be left to lurk around the fridge for too long without reboiling it.

COURT-BOUILLON

There's a hackneyed observation that when someone close dies you recall important things which you kick yourself for not having spoken to them about. When my father died I frisked my brain and came up with nothing. The same when my mother died. Then, about a decade later, it occurred to me that the important thing I had always meant to ask her for was the recipe for the court-bouillon in which she used to cook eels and, sometimes, salmon. This approximation is equally good for veal and chicken.

> WATER
>
> WHITE WINE VINEGAR
>
> WHITE WINE
>
> CELERY
>
> FENNEL
>
> CARROT
>
> LEEK
>
> JUNIPER BERRIES
>
> PEPPERCORNS
>
> CORIANDER SEEDS
>
> MUSTARD SEEDS
>
> CUMIN SEEDS
>
> CARAWAY SEEDS
>
> BAY LEAVES

No one flavour should dominate. Go easy, then, with the wine, the vinegar and the celery.

Bring to the boil then simmer for a couple of hours. Strain thoroughly.

BASICS ARE ON PP. 11–23 … DON'T WALK AWAY … CONCENTRATE … FUCK THE GUESTS … AND ALL THAT CONVIVIALITY MALARKY … DO NOT WASTE BREAD: OIL IT AND REBAKE IT … STOCK! GET TREATMENT FOR SQUEAMISHNESS … VEGETARIANISM IS CURABLE'

The link between literary theft – the unacknowledged stealing of someone else's imaginative work – and the kidnapping and imprisonment of someone else's children, i.e. plagiary, was made by the genitally preoccupied Roman epigrammatist Martial. He bizarrely considered these thefts to be of equal gravity. Literature, we may then deduce, is the product of a generative process. So: we imagine children, therefore we have children. Martial, old son, that's not the way it works.

MIREPOIX / SOFFRITO / SOFRITO X / BATTUTO

A chippy deli owner who was also an unbelievably self-important daytime telly chef once berated Keith Floyd for starting most dishes with a mixture of onions, garlic and so on: he seemed, astonishingly, to believe this had something to do with Keith having been educated at a public school. This ignorant poot might as well have chided every cook in southern Europe, the overwhelming majority of whom had not attended the wrong Wellington.

This is the essential of essentials, the basic of basics. It is the foundation of countless braises, stews, sauces, soups. It is referred to throughout this book as mirepoix. (The name comes from the Duc de Mirepoix who was willingly cuckolded by Louis XV.)

Combine:

ONIONS

GARLIC

CELERY

'SEASON . . . SALT . . . MAYBE PEPPER (CAN BE WHITE) . . . REMOVE THE GERM FROM GARLIC . . . COOK SPICES . . . BOIL OFF ALCOHOL . . . COOK TO PLEASE YOURSELF AS YOU MIGHT WRITE OR PAINT, DANCE OR SING TO PLEASE YOURSELF . . . CREATE YOUR OWN THEFTS . . .

FENNEL

CARROT

SHALLOT

PARSLEY

BAY LEAF

RAW HAM

OLIVE OIL/DUCK FAT

Whatever you're using chop it small. The dominant ingredient should be onion. Celery and carrot should be used with caution. The first is aggressive, the latter sweet. If you are using spices include them at the start. They must be cooked. Don't add them as an afterthought. Cook the mirepoix in olive oil or duck fat for an hour at a low temperature to a point beyond fondant. It should be starting to dissolve.

DUXELLES

MUSHROOMS – CHAMPIGNONS DE PARIS/BUTTON MUSHROOMS

SHALLOTS

ONIONS

BUTTER

Cook the finely chopped shallots and onions in butter till getting soft. Add the equally finely chopped mushrooms and cook slowly for an hour.

BATTER – BASIC

150G FLOUR

20CL WATER

BASICS ARE ON PP. 11–23 ... DON'T WALK AWAY ... CONCENTRATE ... FUCK THE GUESTS ... AND ALL THAT CONVIVALITY MALARKY ... DO NOT WASTE BREAD: OIL IT AND REBAKE IT ... STOCK! GET TREATMENT FOR SQUEAMISHNESS ... VEGETARIANISM IS CURABLE'

I EGG

5CL OLIVE OIL

Beat the egg and oil. Add the sieved flour. Go on beating then pour in the water at a trickle. Cover and leave for an hour or more before using.

BATTER – EVEN MORE BASIC

50G CHICKPEA FLOUR

10CL WATER

SPICES – CHILLI, CUMIN, CINNAMON, ETC.

Sieve the flour. Mix with the powdered spices, add the water to obtain whatever density you require. Set aside for an hour or so.

There is little that is more preposterously comic than one self-important, thick, entirely humourless celebrity chef suing another self-important, thick, entirely humourless celebrity chef for having plagiarised a recipe to which neither self-important, thick, entirely humourless celebrity chef holds the rights. Are there rights to recipes? Maybe to the words that self-important, thick, entirely humourless celebrity chefs (or their ghosts) use but not to the deeds – the dishes – of which those recipes are no more than a blueprint.

'SEASON ... SALT ... MAYBE PEPPER (CAN BE WHITE) ... REMOVE THE GERM FROM GARLIC ... COOK SPICES ... BOIL OFF ALCOHOL ... COOK TO PLEASE YOURSELF AS YOU MIGHT WRITE OR PAINT, DANCE OR SING TO PLEASE YOURSELF ... CREATE YOUR OWN THEFTS ...

SPICES AND A FEW HERBS

Pimenton piccante and the even more ubiquitous **pimenton dulce** from La Vera in Extremadura are powdered peppers dried by smoking – hence their distinctive flavour, familiar from numerous pork products including chorizo. They are the distinguishing flavours of Spain and are to be found in all kitchens save those of pretentious neophiliacs in San Sebastian.

Pimenton from Murcia, again hot or 'sweet', is the product of sun-dried or air-dried peppers and possesses a less complex flavour.

Piment d'Espelette. A mild spice that takes its name from a village in the French Basque country whose hideous spray-on half-timbering is mercifully hidden during those months when strings of peppers are hung from balconies to dry.

Savoury, sarriette, is among the less offensive herbs.

Lovage, livèche, is turbo-charged celery – use with restraint.

Borage leaves can paper-cut your hands. Its flavour recalls cucumber. My grotesquely unjustified and chippy prejudice against it derives from its being a constituent of Pimm's, which I dislike because of its social and, particularly, sartorial associations: braying men in straw hats, shapeless women in all too English hyperfrump, hyperfloral mode.

Ras el hanout is to Morocco what pimenton is to Spain. Unlike pimenton it is a mixture and so varies. Folklore insists that it contain cantharides, the dazzlingly green beetle also known as Spanish fly, which is both an abortifacient and a primitive Viagra – it irritates the genito-urinary tract and dilates blood vessels. Its sale was banned in Morocco in 1990; whether that ban is zealously policed is moot. Ras el hanout is available in supermarkets in the UK and France. It is also easy to blend your own from powders or, if you have a spice grinder, from dried corns, nuts and roots. The essential ingredients are cumin, nutmeg, allspice, chilli, sugar, ginger, cloves, turmeric, black pepper, cinnamon. The inclusion of belladonna, orris root and monk's pepper, all of them associable with witchcraft and the hag's pharmacopoeia, is ill-advised.

Black pepper. While he would undoubtedly have been flattered by the appropriation of his name, it is unlikely that Porfirio Rubirosa would actually have measured up to some of the grinders wielded with menace by leering Italian waiters.

White pepper fell out of fashion in Britain in the trattoria Sixties and has so far failed to make a comeback. Matthew Fort observes in his eye-opening *Eating Up Italy* that Neapolitan cooks favour it – on aesthetic rather than gastronomic grounds. These sensitive souls don't like specks of black pepper showing up in a dish. Nor do I.

Mustard. Dijon: Amora moutarde forte is fine. Avoid the stuff with grains and gimmicks like violet mustard from Brive that is coloured with grape must. English: Colman's is essential for salt beef and pork pies.

Caraway. Powdered for cooking. Crushed for flavouring supermarket own-brand vodka to create kümmel. Whole for eating with Munster, putting in bread, adding to sauerkraut and making potatoes in their jackets just about edible. The most commonly used flavouring in northern Germany, Scandinavia and European Russia after dill (an often unwelcome herb that has to be scraped off dish after dish in Moscow restaurants).

Cumin is akin to caraway; it's sharper, not so sweet, not so pungent.

Saffron is the most delightful, most sexy of spices. And the most expensive. Also the most likely to be pinchbeck, especially if it's powdered, when it may have been cut with turmeric. Use saffron in mayonnaise, risotto, with steamed potatoes, potato purée and white fish.

'SEASON ... SALT ... MAYBE PEPPER (CAN BE WHITE) ... REMOVE THE GERM FROM GARLIC ... COOK SPICES ... BOIL OFF ALCOHOL ... COOK TO PLEASE YOURSELF AS YOU MIGHT WRITE OR PAINT, DANCE OR SING TO PLEASE YOURSELF ... CREATE YOUR OWN THEFTS ...

Cardamom. Imparts a fascinating flavour to milk and cream. Good with rice. The shells are to be discarded. The seeds can either be ground or tied in muslin if being used in a braise.

Orange peel. Dry peel in a low oven for several hours. It can then be powdered or broken into shards. A surprisingly powerful flavouring for stews, braises, etc.

Dried ceps are versatile. The one thing they are not is a substitute for fresh ceps. There's no point in reconstituting them in order to, say, sauté them with garlic. They share little but a name. The dried version is considerably more intense. Their texture renders them more suitable as a flavouring of stocks, long-cooked stews and sauces, and of milk and cream.

Bitter chocolate. A few cubes added to a stew or salmi of red meat or to jugged game have pleasurable results. A few . . . No more.

GARLIC

The writer Charles Dantzig reckons that the British don't get garlic. They used never to use it, now they use too much . . . But then Dantzig abhors Marseille where it is used in reckless abundance.

There are few savoury dishes that don't benefit from its inclusion.

Hit a clove with the side of a knife to get the skin off. When garlic is no longer fresh it develops a green germ that is bitter. It is best removed – cut lengthways down the centre of the clove and remove it with the point of a knife.

If you're adding garlic to something that has been fried – ceps, say, or sauté potatoes – make sure that it doesn't catch. The flavour of burnt garlic is disagreeable and it is liable to contaminate whatever else is in the pan. Do not remove any of the outer skins if you're roasting it, the cloves need as much protection as possible.

BASICS ARE ON PP. 11–23 . . . DON'T WALK AWAY . . . CONCENTRATE . . . FUCK THE GUESTS . . . AND ALL THAT CONVIVALITY MALARKY . . . DO NOT WASTE BREAD: OIL IT AND REBAKE IT . . . STOCK! GET TREATMENT FOR SQUEAMISHNESS . . . VEGETARIANISM IS CURABLE'

OILS, ETC.

'Extra-virgin' might be a desirable quality in nuns – I don't know, I have a horror of these poor women unless they are unsuitably dressed in the films of Walerian Borowczyk and Georges Franju – but applied to olive oil it is close to meaningless. 'Cold pressed' is equally meaningless so indiscriminately is it used. In France a cheap wine used to adulterate another that commands a high price because of its supposed provenance is known as a 'vin médecin'. Though 'huile médecin' has yet to enter the language, the olive oil trade is just as rackety and bent as the wine trade. Which is a boon to those who dislike the peppery throat-assault of the echt product. In olive oil, as in life, the impure is more satisfying than the pure. The sensible course is to buy according to what it tastes like rather than because of the probably mendacious label recounting the history of the terrain, the family, the mill, the artisan tradition and so on.

Flavour with small chillis, peppercorns, coriander seeds, bay leaves, garlic cloves, fennel twigs, mustard seeds, lemon rind, dried tomatoes, etc. Squeeze these into an empty bottle then fill it with oil. Turn the bottle now and again. The oil will take on the properties of the aromatics in a couple of weeks. Keep the bottle topped up.

Various degrees of chastity have spread to other oils:

Walnut. The best in this instance is mere virgin. Distinguished by its brownish colour. (Refined walnut oil is pale, rather insipid.) Because it burns at a low heat its uses are confined to dressings and vinaigrettes. Store in the fridge.

Colza. The fields of England and France are now largely given over to the cultivation of colza or rapeseed. The unrefined oil tastes much better than the fields smell. Both are shrilly yellow. The oil is good for vinaigrettes. Whoever suggested that the flavour recalls newly mown meadows had never set foot in a noisome slurryscape dotted with agri-polythene and oxidised troughs.

'SEASON . . . SALT . . . MAYBE PEPPER (CAN BE WHITE) . . . REMOVE THE GERM FROM GARLIC . . . COOK SPICES . . . BOIL OFF ALCOHOL . . . COOK TO PLEASE YOURSELF AS YOU MIGHT WRITE OR PAINT, DANCE OR SING TO PLEASE YOURSELF . . . CREATE YOUR OWN THEFTS . . .

Toasted sesame. Asian dishes are for consuming, not for preparing. It is futile to steal what you can't understand. And it is presumptuous to cook in a language whose building blocks – its very characters – we do not read or speak. Chinese supermarkets are a delight: an aquarium you can eat, sacks of rice only a forklift can shift, bizarre fruit, marvellous packaging. But I seldom buy anything. This oil is aggressive and of limited use but worth having around till, untouched, it reaches its sell-by. Alternatively, make avocado and sesame paste (p. 32).

Cold pressed sesame. Its relationship to toasted sesame oil is not apparent. I was introduced to it by Nico Ladenis, a chef with a curiosity about cuisines unrelated to that of which he was a consummate master. He was using it to dress something or other. Pour it onto fish, chicken, sweetbreads . . .

Sunflower and peanut. Ideal oils for frying and deep-frying. The better quality ones are components of neutral (or featureless) vinaigrettes.

Duck fat. Much cheaper than goose fat and virtually indistinguishable. A fine medium for chips, sauté potatoes and Pommes Anna.

Butter. Use unsalted butter for all cooking. It burns at a low temperature so, if frying, combine it with sunflower, olive or peanut oil, or duck fat.

Cream. Because I live in France cream means crème fraîche. English double cream's composition may be different but its culinary properties aren't.

Beef dripping. Delicious on toast. A scouser's madeleine. Good for chips and Yorkshire pudding and anything else that comes from north of the Trent.

Plagiarism by anticipation. We make a dish – most likely from leftovers that are at the just-beating heart of culinary improvisation, such as it is – and forget about it, only to discover years later that it is now the ginchiest thing, the talk of the town, etc. Bubble and squeak has been sanctioned by Yannick Grossebite, chef de cuisine at La Chatte Humide in Knutsford, twice winner of the 'Ladies Who Lunch' category in *Cheshire Life*'s annual Restaurant Oscars.

PICADA

Picada is a sauce – sort of. You might eat it without realising it since it is generally stirred into stews, braises and soups just before they are served. It is seldom served separately like rouille, mayonnaise or aïoli. The basis is nuts. It is pretty much peculiar to Catalonia and Valencia. Elsewhere in Spain *picada* means minced meat: there's a small chain of burger and grill restaurants in Madrid called La Vaca Picada, The Minced Cow.

> 6 CLOVES GARLIC
>
> 200G TOASTED HAZELNUTS
>
> 200G TOASTED ALMONDS
>
> 100G PINE NUTS
>
> 200G CROUTONS/MIGAS (P. 148)
>
> 1 SQUARE DARK CHOCOLATE
>
> 1 SMALL GLASS MALAGA OR PEDRO XIMENEZ
>
> 1 TABLESPOONFUL VINEGAR
>
> OLIVE OIL

'SEASON ... SALT ... MAYBE PEPPER (CAN BE WHITE) ... REMOVE THE GERM FROM GARLIC ... COOK SPICES ... BOIL OFF ALCOHOL ... COOK TO PLEASE YOURSELF AS YOU MIGHT WRITE OR PAINT, DANCE OR SING TO PLEASE YOURSELF ... CREATE YOUR OWN THEFTS ...

The nuts, garlic and fried bread need initially to be crushed in a mortar. This will prevent the picada being granular. When they form a paste put them in a processor and gradually add the other ingredients.

SAUCE

HOLLANDAISE

The principle is not much different from that of mayonnaise.

    3 EGG YOLKS

    150G ALMOST MELTED BUTTER

    LEMON JUICE

    WATER

Whisk the eggs with a splash of water and a slug of lemon juice in a bain-marie over just simmering water. Add the butter very gradually, indeed timidly. Never stop whisking.

BEURRE BLANC

Salmon, scallops, veal and most of all pike are enhanced by this wonderful sauce, supposedly the result of a kitchen accident on the banks of the Loire, which may or may not be true. Better surely, though, to 'invent' thus, *from within*, than to sit in the car on the way to work as one of the big name

Alains (Senderens? Ducasse? Passard?) does and confect Regret Rien-style aberrations *from without.*

40G SHALLOTS

20CL DRY WHITE WINE

20CL WHITE WINE VINEGAR

200G BUTTER CUT INTO (MAX) 2CM CUBES AND KEPT VERY COLD

Cut up the shallots as finely as possible. Put them in a pan on a low heat with the wine and the vinegar. Let it reduce till there is hardly a dessert-spoonful of liquid left.

Start to whisk in the butter. Keep at it. When it's all incorporated you can put it through a sieve if you are Doing Fine Dining but this is not a book for fine diners – an anagram of tossers. (I recommend Steven Poole's excellent *You Aren't What You Eat* on this thorny subject.)

TOMATO SAUCE 1

TOMATOES – CANNED OR FRESH OR BOTH

MIREPOIX (P. 14) – MUST INCLUDE GARLIC

PIMENTON PICCANTE

CUMIN

RAS EL HANOUT

OLIVE OIL

(SUGAR – OPTIONAL)

If using fresh tomatoes peel them. Make incisions in the skin, cover them with boiling water. When the skins begin to wrinkle put them into iced water. Remove the skins. Deseed them – strain the seeds and add their liquid to the sauce. Sweat the mirepoix at low heat, adding pimenton piccante, cumin and ras el hanout – these spices must cook. When the mirepoix is thoroughly cooked and the vegetables are soft, add more olive oil, bring up

'SEASON ... SALT ... MAYBE PEPPER (CAN BE WHITE) ... REMOVE THE GERM FROM GARLIC ... COOK SPICES ... BOIL OFF ALCOHOL ... COOK TO PLEASE YOURSELF AS YOU MIGHT WRITE OR PAINT, DANCE OR SING TO PLEASE YOURSELF ... CREATE YOUR OWN THEFTS ...

the heat and add the chopped tomatoes. Stir, then reduce the heat. Cook for 2 hours. Add sugar with care: it may be necessary if you're using fresh tomatoes which tend, in England, to have little flavour.

TOMATO SAUCE 2

The idea here is to retain the flavour of the tomatoes that, with luck, will taste like tomatoes tasted before they stopped tasting of tomatoes and were grown hydroponically in Holland, home of the flavourless.

TOMATOES – FRESH

SHALLOT

SALT

SUNFLOWER OIL

Peel, deseed and chop the tomatoes. Dice the shallot. Soften it in oil. Add the tomatoes. Strain the seeds and add the jelly-like liquid. Cook gently for 20 minutes.

Was Pierre Menard a plagiarist? Yes. But he had a persuasive brief in the form of his creator J. L. Borges.

TOMATO SAUCE 3 / SAUCE VIERGE

TOMATOES – FRESH, RIPE

CHIVES

CORIANDER

OLIVE OIL

LEMON JUICE/PEDRO XIMENEZ VINEGAR

This is closer to a vinaigrette than a sauce. It is not cooked. Peel and deseed the tomatoes. Chop the chives and coriander (which is an improvement on basil). Put in a bowl with the tomatoes and cover with olive oil. Add a small amount of lemon juice or Pedro Ximenez vinegar. Leave in the fridge for 2 or 3 days so that the oil begins to get infused with the flavour of the herbs.

TOMATO SAUCE 4

TOMATOES

OLIVE OIL

SALT

SUGAR

GARLIC CLOVES

STOCK OR COURT-BOUILLON

Cut a large quantity of tomatoes in half. Cover a roasting pan with olive oil. Turn the tomatoes in the oil. Salt them, add a little sugar. Place in a low oven (100°C) and leave for 4–5 hours.

The resultant dried tomatoes will not – or ought not to – resemble the quoits of leather called 'sun-dried tomatoes', which were a dull chewy fashion of the 1980s and are still to be found in exorbitantly priced bottles.

Put these tomatoes into a processor with more olive oil and garlic cloves. Whizz to a paste. The flavour will be intense. It can be kept in the fridge in jars under a duvet of olive oil.

To make a sauce dilute it with light stock or a court-bouillon.

It can obviously be added, too, to stews and braises.

'SEASON ... SALT ... MAYBE PEPPER (CAN BE WHITE) ... REMOVE THE GERM FROM GARLIC ... COOK SPICES ... BOIL OFF ALCOHOL ... COOK TO PLEASE YOURSELF AS YOU MIGHT WRITE OR PAINT, DANCE OR SING TO PLEASE YOURSELF ... CREATE YOUR OWN THEFTS ...

GREEN SAUCE

The combinations and proportions of these ingredients is variable. Even though I'm fond of hard-boiled eggs I believe their incorporation here is inappropriate – a matter of colour once again no doubt. But hard-boiled eggs *with* green sauce/salsa verde/sauce verte is a different matter.

SPINACH

SORREL

SHALLOT

GARLIC

CHIVE

CORIANDER

ROCKET

ANCHOVY

CORNICHONS

CAPERS

VINEGAR

OLIVE OIL

Process the lot apart from the olive oil and vinegar. Add the vinegar, if needed, gingerly. Remember the capers and cornichons have been in vinegar. Add the oil gradually.

No one ingredient should predominate. Indeed it should not be possible to determine what, precisely, it comprises.

PISTOU

Basil is a problem. There are countless varieties; certain are unpleasantly bitter, others almost effervescent on the tongue, some flavourless.

120G BASIL

BASICS ARE ON PP. 11–23 . . . DON'T WALK AWAY . . . CONCENTRATE . . . FUCK THE GUESTS . . . AND ALL THAT CONVIVALITY MALARKY . . . DO NOT WASTE BREAD: OIL IT AND REBAKE IT . . . STOCK! GET TREATMENT FOR SQUEAMISHNESS . . . VEGETARIANISM IS CURABLE'

4 CLOVES GARLIC

15CL OLIVE OIL

Process basil and garlic. Add olive oil in a slow stream.

God made food; the Devil cooks. James Joyce, *Ulysses.*

PESTO

120G BASIL

4 CLOVES GARLIC

30CL OLIVE OIL

30G PINE NUTS

30G PECORINO ROMANO, GRATED

Process everything save the oil into a paste, then add it using the pulse button.

CORIANDER SAUCE

120G CORIANDER LEAVES

15CL SUNFLOWER OIL

JUICE OF 1 LEMON

Process.

'SEASON … SALT … MAYBE PEPPER (CAN BE WHITE) … REMOVE THE GERM FROM GARLIC … COOK SPICES … BOIL OFF ALCOHOL … COOK TO PLEASE YOURSELF AS YOU MIGHT WRITE OR PAINT, DANCE OR SING TO PLEASE YOURSELF … CREATE YOUR OWN THEFTS …

AÏOLI

2 EGG YOLKS

6 CLOVES GARLIC

30CL OLIVE OIL

All ingredients must be at the same (room) temperature.

Make a paste of the yolk and the garlic. Add oil drop by drop, whisking vigorously. Eventually pour it in at a trickle but don't get over-confident. Ultimately the consistency should be almost jelly-like.

BAGNA CAUDA

I.e. hot bath. This is best prepared in large quantities for parties. A baby could have been bathed in the receptacle the Dogliani brothers' cook used. We were in a barn on a hillside among Piedmontese vineyards. It was snowing. Geoffrey Grigson was complaining. His wife Jane was trying to soothe him. There were buckets of Barbera. Paul Levy and Gered Mankowitz were getting stuck into the boiling sauce, which I'd heard of but had never tasted. I had heard too of cardoons, but had never tasted them: I omit them here – too much trouble, and bottled ones are unconvincing. Anyway, the sauce is the thing.

500G UNSALTED BUTTER

50CL OLIVE OIL

SEVERAL TINS OF ANCHOVIES

SEVERAL HEADS OF GARLIC, CHOPPED

Cook the anchovies and garlic cloves over low heat till the latter are soft. Add the butter and oil. Simmer for 30 minutes.

If you have a kitchen equipped with an intern order the wretched creature to prepare cardoons. Otherwise serve with bread, hard-boiled eggs, fennel, beets, endives, grilled and skinned peppers, celery (this is a way of making that raw vegetable palatable).

> Cookbooks feed off cookbooks, fine cuts give way to gruel. Their authors make botched attempts to disguise the sources of their offering. But those familiar with more than half a dozen such books are acquainted with the sensation that *I've read that before in* – where?

AVOCADO AND SESAME PASTE

So far as I can recall I have not eaten guacamole.

AVOCADO

TOASTED SESAME OIL

Remove the skin and stone from the avocado, mash the flesh, gradually incorporate oil. Serve on toast.

CHIMICHURRI

Meat in Argentina is generally of such quality that it doesn't need this sauce, which is nonetheless to be found everywhere.

FLAT LEAF PARSLEY

GARLIC

WHITE WINE VINEGAR

OLIVE OIL

'SEASON . . . SALT . . . MAYBE PEPPER (CAN BE WHITE) . . . REMOVE THE GERM FROM GARLIC . . . COOK SPICES . . . BOIL OFF ALCOHOL . . . COOK TO PLEASE YOURSELF AS YOU MIGHT WRITE OR PAINT, DANCE OR SING TO PLEASE YOURSELF . . . CREATE YOUR OWN THEFTS . . .

Trim the parsley and process with the garlic. Add the olive oil gradually. A splash of vinegar is all that's required. Most recipes include oregano. I dislike the stuff so give it a miss.

AILLADE

Grilled bread rubbed with garlic and moistened with walnut oil is one sort of aillade. A second is a veal (sometimes lamb) stew with a garlicky tomato sauce. A third is this sauce.

Given how peripatetic cooks from the south-west of France are, it is surprising that it has not travelled with them. The Grigson connection here is that Jane asked me at a party whether I still bothered to use cookbooks. I replied truthfully – there's no point in trying to fool a bullshit detector – that I referred to her *Charcuterie and French Pork Cookery* now and again and that I was impressed by the recently published *Cuisine de Terroir*. She too was impressed by it. I was of course smugly delighted to have my taste sanctioned by the great. This suggests that the party in question was in 1988 or '89.

    100G WALNUTS, SHELLED AND PEELED
    50G GARLIC
    30CL WALNUT OIL

Thoroughly blend the walnuts and garlic till a smooth paste is attained – a few drops of water may be needed. Add the oil gradually to start with, as though making an aïoli. The resultant sauce is very rich. It is likely to mug delicately flavoured meat or fish. Spread on bread or serve with raw endive, carrots, fennel, etc.

ANCHOÏADE

250G ANCHOVIES

6 CLOVES GARLIC

25CL OLIVE OIL

Do not drain the oil from the anchovies. Process with the garlic. Add the olive oil gradually.

Spread on toast, fried bread, hard-boiled eggs, raw vegetables, etc. Then there are stuffed tomatoes and courgettes (p. 123).

TAPENADE

250G PITTED BLACK OLIVES

100G CAPERS

25G ANCHOVY FILLETS

6 CLOVES GARLIC

30CL OLIVE OIL

Put everything apart from the olive oil into a processor. When the paste is smooth pour in the oil gradually.

PERSILLADE

GARLIC

FLAT LEAF PARSLEY

Chop finely together.

'SEASON ... SALT ... MAYBE PEPPER (CAN BE WHITE) ... REMOVE THE GERM FROM GARLIC ... COOK SPICES ... BOIL OFF ALCOHOL ... COOK TO PLEASE YOURSELF AS YOU MIGHT WRITE OR PAINT, DANCE OR SING TO PLEASE YOURSELF ... CREATE YOUR OWN THEFTS ...

The successful plagiarist, as both Michel de Montaigne and T. S. Eliot noted, occludes his sources.

Eliot: *We turn first to the parallel quotations from Massinger and Shakespeare collocated by Mr Cruickshank to make manifest Massinger's indebtedness. One of the surest of tests is the way in which a poet borrows. Immature poets imitate; mature poets steal; bad poets deface what they take, and good poets make it into something better, or at least something different. The good poet welds his theft into a whole of feeling which is unique, utterly different from that from which it was torn; the bad poet throws it into something which has no cohesion. A good poet will usually borrow from authors remote in time, or alien in language, or diverse in interest. Chapman borrowed from Seneca; Shakespeare and Webster from Montaigne.*

This is the most celebrated disquisition on plagiarism of the modern age, a truistic observation which has become dictat, quoted as irrefutable fact despite the vocational chasm that divides Shakespeare and Montaigne. Eliot advises that: *The attitude of the craftsman like Shakespeare – whose business was to write plays, not to think – is very different from that of the philosopher or literary critic.* (It should be noted that such *craftsmen* as Joyce and Aragon set little store by thinking before writing.)

Yet Eliot's passage is itself borderline plagiaristic. He reiterated Montaigne who wrote: *I hide my thefts, and disguise them. Others flaunt them. Like a horse thief I paint the mane and tail and sometimes blind them in one eye. If the owner had used it as an ambler I turn it into a trotting horse. And if it was a horse to be saddled and ridden I make a packhorse of it.* I do not hide my thefts. I exhibit an absolute candour about the provenance of this book's content. (That sentence sounds like a lie, and is.) If I know where a recipe comes from I own up to it. However, I don't copy. I steal. Then I make it my own, colour the mane (*la crinière*), which is not to say that I improve it . . . This might be reckoned as criminally coarse as hacking down an exquisite work of, say, Alfred Gilbert and melting it for scrap. So be it. On the other hand, when a recipe has in my opinion been improved by tweaking or the exclusion of certain ingredients, I shall point this out with the falsest modesty known to man.

The book is, further, a deflected meditation on infections of varying gravity: 'influence', 'inspiration', 'homage', 'imitation', Mann's 'higher cribbing', 'channelling' and so on. It proposes that cooking is at best a craft and that craft must always be the same while art must always be different – an unoriginal dictum by the way; it is, of course, Gore Vidal's. (The sort of craft he had in mind was cake-making or scented candle-moulding. He revered Shakespeare as an artist. Beside the haughty desiccated Anglican Eliot, Vidal is a model of humility – that's something that can seldom be said.)

BASICS ARE ON PP. 11–23 . . . DON'T WALK AWAY . . . CONCENTRATE . . . FUCK THE GUESTS . . . AND ALL THAT CONVIVALITY MALARKY . . . DO NOT WASTE BREAD: OIL IT AND REBAKE IT . . . STOCK! GET TREATMENT FOR SQUEAMISHNESS . . . VEGETARIANISM IS CURABLE'

SOUP

STRACCIATELLA

LIGHT STOCK – PREDOMINANTLY CHICKEN

EGGS

PARMESAN OR PECORINO ROMANO

Beat up 1 egg per person. Mix with grated cheese – I prefer Pecorino Romano – to make a light paste. Put a generous dollop of paste in each bowl. Pour on boiling stock.

PASTA E CECI / PASTA AND CHICKPEAS

This one fell off the back of an Alastair Little. It also derives from the version served at Mimi alla Ferrovia in Naples. There is a further correspondence with the Cypriot houmous soup prepared long long ago by the Koritsas family at their delightful café opposite Camden Town underground station.

500G CHICKPEAS

500G PASTA (ROMBI OR PAPPARDELLE)

OLIVE OIL

4 STICKS CELERY

6 CLOVES GARLIC

I HAM BONE

Soak the chickpeas overnight. Cook them for 3 or more hours with the ham bone at a low temperature, just simmering. Sweat the celery and garlic. When they're soft add nearly all the cooked chickpeas. Put the lot through the processor. Use chickpea water and oil to get a soupy consistency. Cook the pasta, add to the soup. Decorate with the remaining chickpeas – or don't bother.

SMOKED HADDOCK SOUP

The restaurant trade likes place names. The supposition is that they legitimise a dish's provenance. A dish then is not a creation, it's *natural, traditional*; like folksongs and oak apple day it just happened to have happened without authorial intervention, parthenogenetically.

This soup is frequently billed as Cullen Skink. Cullen is a Moray sea town. Like its neighbours Keith and Elgin (the Athens of the even further north) it is formally planned and rather grand.

Much of the town is dominated by an immense railway viaduct. From the main street the sea is visible only through one of its arches which is transformed into a proscenium arch. The theatrical magic of this framed aspect recalls de Chirico.

Skinks (haddocks) have, for over a century and a half, been intensively reared in closed weel-puidges to the east of the town. This practice precurses battery farming and is routinely condemned by fish welfare groups such as CBHC. From a culinary point of view there is nothing to distinguish a farmed skink from a free-range one. Nor does vivid yellow dye detract from the flavour even though it is widely regarded as a gastronomic solecism.

'SEASON . . . SALT . . . MAYBE PEPPER (CAN BE WHITE) . . . REMOVE THE GERM FROM GARLIC . . . COOK SPICES . . . BOIL OFF ALCOHOL . . . COOK TO PLEASE YOURSELF AS YOU MIGHT WRITE OR PAINT, DANCE OR SING TO PLEASE YOURSELF . . . CREATE YOUR OWN THEFTS . . .

1KG SMOKED HADDOCK, SKINNED AND BONED

500G FLOURY POTATOES

2L MILK

50CL CREAM

WHITE PEPPER

PINCH OF POWDERED CLOVE, NUTMEG, CINNAMON – GO EASY

Chop haddock and potatoes. Put them in a heavy double boiler with cold milk, cream and pepper.

Heat. Take care. Even with a double boiler there is a chance that it will boil over. What's needed is constant attention and a very douce simmer – not a white apocalypse. Stir frequently. Cook for 25 minutes. The ingredients will have begun to disintegrate. They can be further mashed.

Cooking the haddock for 10 minutes too long might seem excessive. The goal is to infuse everything with the flavour of the smoke.

HARICOT BLANC SOUP

HARICOTS BLANCS

END OF RAW HAM

LIGHT CLEAR STOCK

ONIONS

GARLIC

WHITE LEEK

FENNEL

OLIVE OIL

Soak the haricots overnight. Cook them with the ham bone in chicken stock till soft. Make a white mirepoix (p. 14).

Blend together the beans, the oil and the mirepoix in a mouli or a processor.

Add more strained stock.

Do not decorate.

BASICS ARE ON PP. 11–23 ... DON'T WALK AWAY ... CONCENTRATE ... FUCK THE GUESTS ... AND ALL THAT CONVIVIALITY MALARKY ... DO NOT WASTE BREAD: OIL IT AND REBAKE IT ... STOCK! GET TREATMENT FOR SQUEAMISHNESS ... VEGETARIANISM IS CURABLE'

Craft, then, if it is always to be the same, is necessarily plagiaristic. Originality has no place in the kitchen. Fusion cooking is a sad joke. That is, the deliberate elision (more likely prang) of culinary idioms, of, so to speak, Cyrillic and pictograms. The fusion that comes from colonisation and exploration is different – thus Charentais chaudrée became New England's chowder.

Little ender or big ender, a boiled egg plagiarises the line of boiled eggs going back millennia. Its debt is of a different kind to Swift's putting into Gulliver's mouth words that have been plundered verbatim from *Mariner's Magazine*. Or Sterne's nifty effrontery in denouncing plagiarism in words stolen from Robert Burton – surely a gag precursive of Duchamp. He was waiting to get found out. Which he wasn't, till after his death.

HAMBURGER SAURE SUPPE > AALSUPPE

The combination of sweet and savoury flavours may seem odd to the English palate but is commonplace in northern Germany where, for instance, plums are served with meat, rhubarb with fish, and broths are flavoured with dried berries. This recipe is broadly based on that given by Alan Davidson in *North Atlantic Seafood*. However it omits the dumplings which Davidson prescribes and includes gingerbread and black bread which is the practice of a strenuously gemütlich restaurant in Altona whose name I forget.

END OF RAW HAM

CELERIAC

CARROTS

'SEASON . . . SALT . . . MAYBE PEPPER (CAN BE WHITE) . . . REMOVE THE GERM FROM GARLIC . . . COOK SPICES . . . BOIL OFF ALCOHOL . . . COOK TO PLEASE YOURSELF AS YOU MIGHT WRITE OR PAINT, DANCE OR SING TO PLEASE YOURSELF . . . CREATE YOUR OWN THEFTS . . .

LEEKS

PRUNES

SULTANAS

DRIED PEARS

DRIED APRICOTS

CARAWAY SEEDS

JUNIPER BERRIES

CLOVES

BLACK BREAD

GINGERBREAD

VINEGAR

BROWN SUGAR

(POACHED EEL (P. 64) – OPTIONAL)

Cook the end of ham in 2 litres of water with the juniper berries and caraway seeds. Skim. After an hour discard the berries and seeds and remove the meat from the bone. Return it to its now reduced cooking liquid with the chopped vegetables and the dried fruit. Cook for a further 40 minutes. Add crumbled gingerbread and diced black bread; adjust the flavour with vinegar and sugar.

(Put in the pieces of eel previously cooked in court-bouillon and heat them through. This addition transforms saure suppe into aalsuppe.)

JERUSALEM ARTICHOKE SOUP

These tubers are neither artichokes nor connected to Jerusalem. They are a bore to peel. But their flavour is unlike anything else. An intern is once again useful.

JERUSALEM ARTICHOKES

LIGHT STOCK

BASICS ARE ON PP. 11–23 . . . DON'T WALK AWAY . . . CONCENTRATE . . . FUCK THE GUESTS . . . AND ALL THAT CONVIVIALITY MALARKY . . . DO NOT WASTE BREAD: OIL IT AND REBAKE IT . . . STOCK! GET TREATMENT FOR SQUEAMISHNESS . . . VEGETARIANISM IS CURABLE'

Steam the peeled and thinly sliced artichokes. Put them through a mouli then into a pan. Add stock. Cook at a simmer for half an hour.

In Adelaide in 1986, Alain Robbe-Grillet, wearing a rumpled safari suit, announced to Craig Raine and Cabrera Infante that *Je suis voleur*. He was saying just the opposite. And he knew that they knew: the most original prose writer of the second half of the 20th century could get away with any number of false confessions because that prose seemed to start at year zero.

No genuine literary thief would ever dare make so shameful an admission. The genuine thief fears exposure. The genuine thief secretly craves exposure. For him theft is a creative act that obliterates his imaginative poverty, a creative act he wishes to be acknowledged.

CAULIFLOWER SOUP

1 CAULIFLOWER

3 LARGE FLOURY POTATOES

1 ONION

150CL MILK

2 EGG YOLKS

CREAM

NUTMEG

Excise the tougher bit of cauliflower stem. Chop the rest of it and blanch it.

Put it to boil in fresh water, gently, with the quartered onion. Boil the potatoes in another pan. When the cauliflower and onion are soft put them

'SEASON ... SALT ... MAYBE PEPPER (CAN BE WHITE) ... REMOVE THE GERM FROM GARLIC ... COOK SPICES ... BOIL OFF ALCOHOL ... COOK TO PLEASE YOURSELF AS YOU MIGHT WRITE OR PAINT, DANCE OR SING TO PLEASE YOURSELF ... CREATE YOUR OWN THEFTS ...

through a processor. When the potato is ready put it through a mouli. Put them together in a pan to cook with the milk. Don't let it boil over. Cook for an age. Add cream to thicken, nutmeg to revert to childhood, beaten eggs yolks to enrichen.

FENNEL SOUP

This delicious slightly sweet soup was serendipitous. Half-inched from Chance, then. I became absorbed in a football match I had expected to be a disappointment so forgot to check the bulbs I was braising. But I inadvertently timed my run to perfection and got to the pot before it had caught. The thinly sliced fennel had melted.

    6 FENNEL BULBS
    75CL LIGHT STOCK
    (25CL CREAM)
    BUTTER
    OLIVE OIL

In a pan with a lid sweat the thinly sliced fennel in butter, oil and 10cl stock for 90 minutes at least. Process it. Add the remaining stock and the cream, maybe.

Cooking can never actually fulfil its obligation to plagiarise because the just cooked plagiarised dish is sloping through someone's digestive tract and the next time it is cooked it will be with fresh ingredients (unless we are discussing a coprophagic cycle).

ALMOND SOUP

The genuine article bulks out the almonds with almost as much bread. This dilutes the flavour of the almonds. So forget about the genuine article. Forget too about including grapes and vinegar.

> 350G BLANCHED ALMONDS
>
> 4 CLOVES GARLIC
>
> 75CL ICED WATER
>
> 15CL SUNFLOWER OIL

Process the almonds and garlic to a dry mass that sticks to the sides of the bowl. Scrape into the centre of the bowl. Add water gradually till you have a soup-like consistency. Add sunflower oil (olive oil overpowers the almonds). Serve very cold.

CUCUMBER SOUP

> 2 CUCUMBERS
>
> 75CL CAILLÉ OR SHEEP YOGHURT OR GOAT YOGHURT
>
> MINT
>
> ICED WATER
>
> COLZA OIL

Peel and deseed the cucumber. Put it in the processor with whichever lactic product you choose and blast it. Caillé is fermented and very light, of Basque origin, at the far end of the spectrum from Greek yoghurt. Adjust the texture with water and a drop or two of colza oil. Add chopped mint if you fancy it, but not much. Serve chilled.

'SEASON ... SALT ... MAYBE PEPPER (CAN BE WHITE) ... REMOVE THE GERM FROM GARLIC ... COOK SPICES ... BOIL OFF ALCOHOL ... COOK TO PLEASE YOURSELF AS YOU MIGHT WRITE OR PAINT, DANCE OR SING TO PLEASE YOURSELF ... CREATE YOUR OWN THEFTS ...

The Tichborne Claimant, Perkin Warbeck, Lambert Simnel . . . Usurpers and pretenders are plagiarists whose creation is themselves.

EGG

DEEP-FRIED EGGS

A childhood treat.

Do not try it if you are not confident about domestic deep-frying. My mother was overconfident: she had a certain expertise in setting light to kitchens.

A wok, an implement I seldom use, is handy. You will also need a slotted spoon and 2 large shallow wooden spoons.

EGGS

PEANUT OIL

The oil must be hot. Put the wooden spoons in the oil to heat them so that the eggs don't stick to them. Do eggs one at a time. Break an egg into a bowl. Slide the egg into the oil. Immediately begin to bathe the exposed side with bubbling oil and cover the yolk with albumen – come at it from both directions with the shallow spoons. Give it 20 seconds then turn the egg over. The side which has been lower will be brown and frilly. Another 20 seconds – then lift it out with a slotted spoon. Degrease on kitchen roll.

BASICS ARE ON PP. 11–23 . . . DON'T WALK AWAY . . . CONCENTRATE . . . FUCK THE GUESTS . . . AND ALL THAT CONVIVIALITY MALARKY . . . DO NOT WASTE BREAD: OIL IT AND REBAKE IT . . . STOCK! GET TREATMENT FOR SQUEAMISHNESS . . . VEGETARIANISM IS CURABLE'

EGGS, SOFT-BOILED AND FRIED

4 EGGS

1 BEATEN EGG

VINEGAR

FLOUR

FINE BREADCRUMBS

Boil eggs for a bare 4 minutes in vinegary water (this makes removing the shell easier). Take them out and put them into cold water with ice cubes to stop them cooking. Peel off the shell. Roll the eggs in flour. Then in beaten egg. Then in breadcrumbs. Fry fairly gently in butter till the breadcrumbs are well coloured. Take great care when turning them.

The cook's duty is to plagiarise. If the cook doesn't plagiarise he is forced to invent. And invention has no place in cooking. However, cryptomnesia – the conviction that we have invented what we have unwittingly lifted from elsewhere – has a paramount part to play.

TORTILLA

1KG POTATOES

500G ONIONS

8 CLOVES GARLIC

8 EGGS

25CL CREAM

PIMENTON PICCANTE

'SEASON ... SALT ... MAYBE PEPPER (CAN BE WHITE) ... REMOVE THE GERM FROM GARLIC ... COOK SPICES ... BOIL OFF ALCOHOL ... COOK TO PLEASE YOURSELF AS YOU MIGHT WRITE OR PAINT, DANCE OR SING TO PLEASE YOURSELF ... CREATE YOUR OWN THEFTS ...

Sweat the sliced onions, garlic and potatoes with pimenton in olive oil in a pan with a lid. The potatoes must fry without taking on colour and developing a crust – so control the cooking with the lid which, when affixed, will cause them to steam. Beat the eggs and cream. Add the potato and onion mix. Oil a pan deep enough to allow the tortilla to rise. Cook in the oven at about 150°C so that it doesn't stick. After 20 minutes turn over the tortilla into a second oiled pan. This can be tricky. Be patient.

CHEESE SOUFFLÉ

Soufflés gain nothing from being made with flour.

6 EGGS

100G COMTÉ

50G PECORINO ROMANO OR PARMESAN

BUTTER

Butter a high-sided vessel – the raw soufflé mix should not come more than two-thirds of the way up the sides. Preheat oven to 200°C. Separate the eggs. If you fuck up do not chance it by including broken yolk in the albumen, it'll prevent it stiffening. Grate the cheese finely. Mix all of the Comté and 40g of the Pecorino with the beaten yolks. Whisk the egg whites till they are sufficiently stiff to form peaks. Fold the whites into the yolk and cheese mix. Do not get too thorough, the whites must retain their airiness – the thing you are constructing is, after all, called a breath. Powder the top with the remaining Pecorino. Cook for 30–35 minutes. Serve immediately.

―――――――――――

I would not exchange my favourite fare (bacon and eggs, beer) for the most misspelt menu in the world. Vladimir Nabokov.

Not sure about that word 'fare'.

―――――――――――

TRIPLE SEC SOUFFLÉ

6 EGGS

120G ICING SUGAR

10CL COINTREAU

BUTTER

Butter and sugar a high-sided vessel – the raw soufflé mix should not come more than two-thirds of the way up the sides. Preheat oven to 200°C. Separate the eggs. If you fuck up do not chance it by including broken yolk in the albumen, it'll prevent it stiffening. Mix 110g of the sugar with the Cointreau and beaten yolks. Whisk the whites till they are stiff. Fold the whites into the yolk mix. Powder the top with the remaining sugar. Cook for 30–35 minutes. Serve immediately.

ROTHSCHILD SOUFFLÉ

Follow the Triple Sec recipe adding chopped glacé fruits to the yolks and Cointreau. Cut the amount of sugar accordingly.

SABAYON / ZABAGLIONE

It was a photograph in *Nova*, a thrilling magazine to a teenage boy, which prompted me to first attempt this, to show off to a teenage girl. In the mid-Sixties it had become suddenly fashionable for men to cook: the ability to do something other than a fry-up was as essential as a twin-tab collar shirt, a tonic suit and a pack of Gitanes. I blame Len Deighton.

4 EGG YOLKS

60G SUGAR

'SEASON . . . SALT . . . MAYBE PEPPER (CAN BE WHITE) . . . REMOVE THE GERM FROM GARLIC . . . COOK SPICES . . . BOIL OFF ALCOHOL . . . COOK TO PLEASE YOURSELF AS YOU MIGHT WRITE OR PAINT, DANCE OR SING TO PLEASE YOURSELF . . . CREATE YOUR OWN THEFTS . . .

ORANGE ZEST

MARSALA OR PEDRO XIMENEZ, LOUPIAC, MONBAZILLAC

Whisk the yolks and sugar in a bowl over hot, but not quite boiling, water. Whisk in opposite directions. The mixture will gradually thicken and pale. Grate in some orange zest. Add a small glass of sweet wine. Serve warm, immediately.

'Turnitin' is an 'originality checker' that determines what has been stolen/borrowed/unknowingly 'remembered' in academic papers.

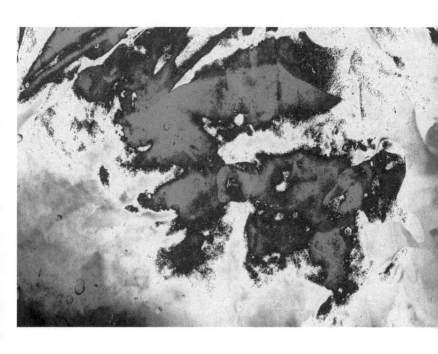

FISH

GRILLED MACKEREL

MACKEREL

The fish must be extremely fresh. It needs 4–5 minutes each side on/under a very hot grill. Do not add any sort of sauce. Just salt.

BOUFFI / BLOATER

The word means swollen in both languages: in French this lightly smoked ungutted herring is also known as a gendarme. They are obtainable from the Cley Smokehouse in north Norfolk, the Fish Society and J. C. David in Boulogne sur Mer.

BOUFFI

WATER

Boil water to cover the fish in a receptacle big enough to take it without bending it. When the water hits boiling point turn it off and put in the fish. Leave it for 10 minutes – this is also the best way to 'cook' kippers which, given that they were both once herrings, are really not much like bouffis. Patience is required to fillet them. Skin them first – most of the skin will have come off in the hot water. Then separate the fillets at the seams. They require no accompaniment save, perhaps, buttered black bread. The prize, the *sot-l'y-laisse*, is the roe. If its most potent flavour seems a bit much it can be made into a paste, diluted with butter and cream.

MATJES HERRING

Matjes are herrings caught before they have spawned. They are reputedly at their best in early summer when stalls appear on Amsterdam streets. Matjes made the Hansa. Seven centuries later they are still consumed voraciously in Bremen, Stralsund, Rostock and in Hamburg whose Sunday morning fish market is a temple of greed. All that is needed with them are raw onions and akvavit or Hamburger kümmel. Never make the mistake of ordering a Rostocker kümmel in Hamburg: it's akin to marching into a Celtic pub singing *The Billy Boys*.

SKATE WITH BROWN BUTTER

4 SKATE WINGS

120G BUTTER

10CL VINEGAR

20G CAPERS

Poach skate wings in salted water for 6 or 7 minutes.

Meanwhile cook the butter till almost brown, then add sweet vinegar – Chardonnay or Pedro Ximenez – and capers. Bring this to a boil. Pour over the drained fish.

'SEASON ... SALT ... MAYBE PEPPER (CAN BE WHITE) ... REMOVE THE GERM FROM GARLIC ... COOK SPICES ... BOIL OFF ALCOHOL ... COOK TO PLEASE YOURSELF AS YOU MIGHT WRITE OR PAINT, DANCE OR SING TO PLEASE YOURSELF ... CREATE YOUR OWN THEFTS ...

Has no one in this country got a Jewish mother? On his first visit to that country Bernard Levin laments Israeli cooking. The point of course is that he associated Jewish cooking with the Ashkenazi tradition while Israel's is predominantly Sephardi. The further point is that we expect what we know. Our anticipation is heightened by the promise of the familiar.

SALMON TARTAR

2 SALMON FILLETS

CREAM

TOASTED SESAME OIL

CHIVES

CORIANDER

WHITE PEPPER

Cut off the salmon skin. Dice the fish. Mix with chopped chives and coriander, a little cream and a bit more oil. A touch of white pepper. Put in the fridge for at least an hour.

Fry the salmon skin till crisp in hot oil infused with chilli. Drain it. Break it into shards and scatter on the cold tartar.

SALMON WITH TAPENADE CRUST

SALMON FILLET

TAPENADE (P. 34)

Smear salmon fillets with tapenade about 5mm thick.

Put in an oiled dish and cook in a hot oven, 240°C, for 8 minutes maximum.

SALMON WITH TAPENADE AND YOGHURT

SALMON FILLET

GOAT YOGHURT

TAPENADE (P. 34)

Mix equal quantities of yoghurt and tapenade to make a mid-grey ointment. Heat very gently in a saucepan, do not let it boil.

Poach salmon fillets in a hardly trembling court-bouillon (p. 13) for 10 minutes. Pour the sauce partly over them. The combination of grey and pink is a pleasing addition to the repertoire of pale dishes.

Marco Pierre White – like any good cook constantly all about trout for dishes to nick – liberated this one, amending the sauce to a black olive beurre blanc.

SALMON IN JELLY

SALMON FILLET

STOCK (CHICKEN OR VEAL)

The stock must be gelatinous and savoury. It must also be clear of particulates. Strain through muslin and strain again. Boil enough to easily cover the salmon fillets. Put the fillets into the bowl they will be served from. Pour the boiling stock onto the fish. Leave to cool then put in the fridge till the jelly has set.

'SEASON ... SALT ... MAYBE PEPPER (CAN BE WHITE) ... REMOVE THE GERM FROM GARLIC ... COOK SPICES ... BOIL OFF ALCOHOL ... COOK TO PLEASE YOURSELF AS YOU MIGHT WRITE OR PAINT, DANCE OR SING TO PLEASE YOURSELF ... CREATE YOUR OWN THEFTS ...

There's not a great deal to admire about Richard John Bingham, 7th Earl of Lucan: a dim, gullible patsy who was no better at uxoricide than at gambling. His diet was so fabulously unimaginative that it was a thing of wonder. He lunched in his club. Every day in winter he ate smoked salmon and lamb cutlets. Every day in summer he ate smoked salmon and lamb cutlets *en gelée*. A few miles and a world away, in Kilburn, a building labourer enjoyed a similarly repetitive diet of, exclusively, Guinness and potato crisps. His was one of the last cases of scurvy to be notified in the UK.

SALTED SALMON

Volgograd: a city of alarming poverty where the sky is pink, green, orange or blue according to which chimney is, at that moment, the most assiduous pollutant. A city too of alarming wealth. Teenage lotharios in Ferraris cruise the avenues with their expensive escorts. They make a big thing of being seen to park their snarling boasts on the pavements in front of outdoor restaurants. Rebels! Impressive!

At one such restaurant near the broad, kitsch-classical stairs down to the river the menu proposes salad of cancer necks and salmon salty. The former is of course a crab salad – the cancer bit is easy, it's the necks that are bemusing. And the latter is merely salmon that has been salted, gravadlax.

> SALMON FILLETS – IT DOESN'T MATTER WHETHER OR NOT
> THEY ARE SKINNED
>
> SALT
>
> SUGAR
>
> WHITE PEPPER
>
> PIMENT D'ESPELETTE

BASICS ARE ON PP. 11–23 ... DON'T WALK AWAY ... CONCENTRATE ... FUCK THE GUESTS ... AND ALL THAT CONVIVIALITY MALARKY ... DO NOT WASTE BREAD: OIL IT AND REBAKE IT ... STOCK! GET TREATMENT FOR SQUEAMISHNESS ... VEGETARIANISM IS CURABLE'

In a bowl of a size appropriate to the amount of salmon, mix the 'cure', enough to cover the salmon. Go easy on the sugar.

Dry the salmon with kitchen roll. Put it too in the bowl so that every surface is covered. Seal the bowl with clingfilm. Put in a fridge for at least 48 hours.

Rinse the salmon thoroughly – it will have released a lot of moisture. Dry it. Eat it raw, sliced thinly. Or steam it for about 8–10 minutes. This is a method Jeremy Lee employs at Quo Vadis; it is superb. Either way, don't smother it with dill or mustard or, worse, both of them.

COULIBIAC

This is essentially a layered pie/pirog. It is among the vernacular Russian dishes that were refined to gluttonous excess by French chefs at St Petersburg in the early 19th century. The French of course claim it as their own, though the Caucasian pastry is not otherwise part of the French repertoire and nor are kasha and vesiga, which you'll be lucky to find – nonetheless, try.

KHATCHAPURI DOUGH (P. 158)

PRE-TOASTED KASHA OR PILAU RICE

6 SALMON FILLETS, ABOUT 10CM LONG

SOFT HERRING ROES, I.E. MILTS (SPERM SACS)

VESIGA (DRIED SPINAL CHORD OF STURGEON)

HARD-BOILED EGGS

DUXELLES (P. 15)

DILL (?)

SPINACH OR SORREL OR A MIX OF THE TWO

LEMON BUTTER

Knead and refrigerate enough dough to provide two sheets of 30cm × 20cm.

Steam the salmon briefly, so that it's far from cooked.

Steam the spinach/sorrel leaves, then rigorously squeeze out all the liquid till dry.

'SEASON ... SALT ... MAYBE PEPPER (CAN BE WHITE) ... REMOVE THE GERM FROM GARLIC ... COOK SPICES ... BOIL OFF ALCOHOL ... COOK TO PLEASE YOURSELF AS YOU MIGHT WRITE OR PAINT, DANCE OR SING TO PLEASE YOURSELF ... CREATE YOUR OWN THEFTS ...

Cook the kasha or pilau rice (which needs to be lightly coloured in butter or oil). Then the same method and quantities for both: 250g to 45cl water or stock (and multiples thereof). Bring to the boil in a lidded pan, lower heat for 15 minutes, leave in pan off heat for a further 5 minutes. All liquid must be absorbed.

Everything needs to be cold before the pie can be composed.

Cover the bottom sheet of dough, save the edges, with half the spinach/sorrel – the idea is to protect the pastry from the liquids produced by the various ingredients. Then a layer of half the duxelles. Then salmon with minced dill, but do go very easy with that aggressive herb – indeed, maybe omit it. Sliced hard-boiled eggs come next followed by the herring roes. Penultimate, more duxelles. Last, the rest of the spinach/sorrel.

Now cover with the second sheet of dough. Crimp the edges. Make a few incisions in the top and brush it with egg yolk. Cook at about 180°C for 40 minutes. Serve with lemon butter.

Where the vesiga would fit in is moot.

Unbound is offering a prize of a night's entertainment with no fewer than three highly experienced, oligarch-tested milt extractors to anyone who can track down vesiga in the UK.

BRANDADE DE MORUE

500G SALT COD

30CL OLIVE OIL OR WALNUT OIL

Desalinate the cod for 24 hours or more in deep water with frequent changes of water.

Cover in cold water and bring to the boil. As soon as it has boiled take it off the heat. Leave it to cool a bit. Take out all the bones – this may require a knife as well as tweezers. Strip off the skin.

Put the fish into a processor. Whizz. Gradually add the oil. Eat on croutons.

The inevitable dispute with this preparation is about whether or not garlic should be included. Sometimes I do, sometimes I don't. Depending on the fish the flavour can vary between assertive and delicate. Check before adding garlic.

ACCRAS DE MORUE

400G SALT COD

200G POTATO

20CL OLIVE OIL

4 CLOVES GARLIC

PARSLEY WITHOUT STALKS

PIMENTON PICCANTE

Boil the potatoes, put them through a mouli or ricer and into a bowl.

Proceed as above for the cod till you reach the processor stage. Whizz. But add only a very little oil. Remove from the processor and put into the bowl with the potatoes, crushed garlic and chopped parsley. Mix together, adding oil only to ease the homogenisation. The aim is to achieve a stiff paste that can be formed by hand into globes a bit larger than a squash ball. Fry them in hot oil to which pimenton piccante has been added.

———

There can never be too little on a plate. Kingsley Amis advised that the three most depressing words in the language were *red or white*. Good try. So is *new comedy series* a good try. But the laurels must surely go to *all the trimmings*. A domestic cook cannot possibly do justice to the array of vegetables, tubers, Yorkshire pudding and prunes wrapped in bacon that anti-gastronomic 'tradition' decrees.

In Italy if you order beef tongue that is what you get – beef tongue. Which is elegant in its solitude. What is garnish if not a distraction from the paucity of the main

'SEASON . . . SALT . . . MAYBE PEPPER (CAN BE WHITE) . . . REMOVE THE GERM FROM GARLIC . . . COOK SPICES . . . BOIL OFF ALCOHOL . . . COOK TO PLEASE YOURSELF AS YOU MIGHT WRITE OR PAINT, DANCE OR SING TO PLEASE YOURSELF . . . CREATE YOUR OWN THEFTS . . .

piece? So, no garnish. And, usually, no accompaniment or only a minimal accompaniment. I have then made very few 'serving suggestions', preferring to eat one thing at a time. The presence of the conjunction *with* in recipe titles or on menus is disheartening. Most foods are not improved by being wedded or civil partnered with others.

EEL

Catch your eel. No, don't. The nature of many tidal rivers is changing because of laissez-faire management and greed. The riverine meadows and narrow watercourses where eels once flourished are being drained to make them agriculturally utile. Subsidies! Eels are slaughtered by the hydro systems that effect this drainage. Try then to get 'farmed' eels. You don't have to pay through the nose. Chinese supermarkets are a good bet. The astonishing SeeWoo, between Greenwich and Charlton, has the most attractive aquarium I've ever seen – you can eat it. Mick Jenrick in Billingsgate Market supposedly sells only wholesale quantities, *very early in the morning*. Worth a punt. So too is Birmingham fish market.

My father had an (illegal) eel trap at the bottom of the garden, where the Nadder joins the Hampshire Avon. In spring I'd be invited to jump into the still wintry river, sling ropes under the trap, then get back onto the bank to help haul it out with the creatures squirming within the chicken-wire-and-bicycle-wheel structure, an ad-hoc version of the telescopic nets used by professional fishermen on the Tamar, the Wye and the Severn.

To kill an eel you need a brick and a concrete surface. Hit it on the head. Then hit it again. To skin it, nail it by what remains of its head to a rough wooden work surface. Cut round the skin just below the head then make incisions to loosen the skin. This should allow you to grip the skin with the aid of a cloth or a gardening glove and pull it off. *Should* allow you: it's not a straightforward process, bear with it.

Once you have removed the skin make a slit from head to tail in order to eviscerate it. Easy enough if you're not squeamish. I should point out that no matter how thoroughly you've bashed its head in – think here of old Phillip Mathers – the eel is going to be wriggling in its posthumous throes.

The following are the three means of preparation my parents used. In each of them the eels should be cut into pieces 4 or 5cm long.

Eels, fried

Dust eel pieces in seasoned flour – pepper, cayenne, turmeric, etc.

Lightly oil the pan or brush it with dripping: eels are fat, naturally 'self-basting'. Cook them for 8–10 minutes.

Eels, grilled

The barbecue was an oil drum brazier with a wire grill across it. Various herbs would get thrown on, mainly bay leaves and rosemary. Cook for 10 minutes.

Eels, poached

Poach the eels in court-bouillon (p. 13) for about 7 minutes at an unhurried simmer. Eels done this way are fabulously succulent.

Sauce is not necessary but if you must . . . then try this *sage cream* which Detlev Schmidkunz used to serve with eels at Kreutzer in Regensburg.

CREAM

SAGE

Bring to the boil a saucepan of cream with a big bunch of sage in it. Lower the heat and cook for an hour, by which time the cream will have reduced and will have been infused with the flavour of the herb. Which you remove and chuck.

When poached eel is added to saure suppe it becomes Hamburger aalsuppe (p. 42).

'SEASON . . . SALT . . . MAYBE PEPPER (CAN BE WHITE) . . . REMOVE THE GERM FROM GARLIC . . . COOK SPICES . . . BOIL OFF ALCOHOL . . . COOK TO PLEASE YOURSELF AS YOU MIGHT WRITE OR PAINT, DANCE OR SING TO PLEASE YOURSELF . . . CREATE YOUR OWN THEFTS . . .

PIKE WITH BEURRE BLANC

Pike are glorious creatures, sinister, streamlined, fierce, cunning. The way they loiter in thick venusian weeds on the *qui vive* for prey is something to behold. Those from sluggish streams and flatland canals are not worth eating. They can never be wholly purged of the taint of silt and sump, never absolved of being bottom feeders. Pike from a chalk stream are a different matter.

My father's characterisation of pike as 'hot cotton wool with needles in it' was born out of experience of bad cooking or of hearing of bad cooking. It was also symptomatic of England's silly, anti-gastronomic hierarchy that elevated 'game' fish above 'coarse' fish and was prejudicial to the latter. Further, a pike is notoriously difficult to debone. The first time I did it was with the aid (not really the word) of a series of diagrams in a magazine printed on the coarse paper of the late 1940s. It took hours. Now there are outdoorsy tutorials on the web, most of them conducted by Canadians, some of them francophone with the extraordinary accent of the Quebecois backwoods. Equip yourself with an electric fillet knife, or 'flay' knife as anglophone Canadians call it. These deafeningly camouflaged, survivalist, bulk-moustached gutting-operatives make it look easy; but, then, it is their life.

The fish's flavour is rich yet delicate and sweet – the only sweet thing about it. The Lyonnais preparation of a panada mixed with the flesh is a labour-intensive means of making a small amount of flesh go a long way. Once it is napped (chefspeak for swamped) with sauce Nantua, as it is in countless bouchons, the flavour is all but undetectable. The sauce takes its name from a lake on the edge of the Jura. Although it is meant to comprise béchamel and crayfish butter it is frequently indistinguishable from an over-reduced generic shellfish soup.

This equally traditional, supposedly Nantais, preparation is much more like it.

PIKE FILLETS

COURT-BOUILLON (P. 13)

BEURRE BLANC (P. 25)

BASICS ARE ON PP. 11–23 . . . DON'T WALK AWAY . . . CONCENTRATE . . . FUCK THE GUESTS . . . AND ALL THAT CONVIVIALITY MALARKY . . . DO NOT WASTE BREAD: OIL IT AND REBAKE IT . . . STOCK! GET TREATMENT FOR SQUEAMISHNESS . . . VEGETARIANISM IS CURABLE'

Timing is important. Poach the fillets in the barely bubbling court-bouillon for 10 minutes.

Prepare the beurre blanc so that it is ready just as the pike is. This is a sauce that can't wait around.

The only pike dish I've eaten that matches this was one served at L'Auberge Fleurie in the remote Avesnois village of Sars Poteries near the Belgian border. Its ethereal sauce was based on genièvre from the Persyn distillery at Houlle, a liquor whose juniper flavour is more pronounced than that of English gins (save, maybe, Plymouth). This is a rough approximation.

25CL CREAM

20 JUNIPER BERRIES

20CL PLYMOUTH GIN, GENIÈVRE OR PEKET (THE WALLOON NAME)

10CL COURT-BOUILLON

Bring the lot to the boil, turn down low and reduce by three-quarters.

LAX PUDDING

The 1980s: Anna's Place was a front-room restaurant somewhere between Islington and Dalston off the Balls Pond Road (home of The Honeycombs). The 'new' Scandinavian cooking (berries, grasses, seaweed, etc.) was far in the future. The 'old' Scandinavian cooking was heartening in its immutability. Outside the apes of Noma it still is. Witness Copenhagen's splendid food market where little changes from year to year. Witness, on the other hand, the Norwegian conviction that jacket potatoes represent some sort of culinary peak – not so heartening. This was among several excellent dishes that the restaurant offered. The recipe is mostly guesswork.

1KG WAXY POTATOES

500G SALTED SALMON (P. 59)

'SEASON . . . SALT . . . MAYBE PEPPER (CAN BE WHITE) . . . REMOVE THE GERM FROM GARLIC . . . COOK SPICES . . . BOIL OFF ALCOHOL . . . COOK TO PLEASE YOURSELF AS YOU MIGHT WRITE OR PAINT, DANCE OR SING TO PLEASE YOURSELF . . . CREATE YOUR OWN THEFTS . . .

50CL CREAM

BUTTER

Slice the potatoes and the salmon 3mm thick. Layer potatoes, cream, salmon in a buttered gratin dish. Repeat. Repeat. Cook for 40–50 minutes at 200°C.

JANSSON'S TEMPTATION

1KG WAXY POTATOES

500G ONIONS

250G ANCHOVY FILLETS

60CL CREAM

BUTTER

Cook the sliced onions till they are soft. Layer them with sliced potatoes, anchovies and cream in a buttered gratin dish. Repeat. Repeat. Bake for 40–50 minutes at 200°C. The 'real', 'authentic' dish used sprats. Stick with the unreal.

Nothing needs re-interpreting. Nothing needs a 'twist'. The wheel has already been invented. The best a cook can do is to improve on what's there – that usually means stripping out redundant ingredients. It means going back to the very foundations, of starting from zero in order to reach a point that has been reached many times before.

BASICS ARE ON PP. 11–23 ... DON'T WALK AWAY ... CONCENTRATE ... FUCK THE GUESTS ... AND ALL THAT CONVIVALITY MALARKY ... DO NOT WASTE BREAD: OIL IT AND REBAKE IT ... STOCK! GET TREATMENT FOR SQUEAMISHNESS ... VEGETARIANISM IS CURABLE'

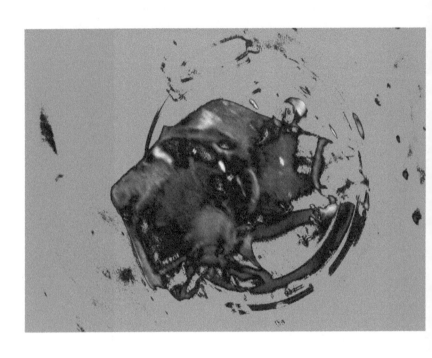

MEAT

SPATCHCOCKED CHICKEN

This ancient method is unquestionably the best way to *roast* chicken (and duck and guinea fowl) even though it was originally devised for grilling.

The heavier, sharper and (probably) the more expensive the poultry shears you use the easier it will be. First excise the backbone, cutting along both sides of it. Cut down into the breastbone. Break the legs and wings. Exert as much downward pressure as possible – remember, it is dead, it doesn't care how rough your love is. The chicken should now be flattened. There are numerous online demonstrations but it's simple stuff.

CHICKEN

OLIVE OIL

SALTED LEMON

SPICES – RAS EL HANOUT, PIMENTON PICCANTE, CINNAMON, CUMIN

Oil the bird thoroughly, skin, cavities, the lot. Spice it thoroughly. Cut salted lemon into tiny dice and push under the skin here and there. Put on a rack in a meat tray.

Cook at 220°C for 40–50 minutes, turning every 10 or so minutes. All the skin will be very crisp, the flesh moist. Deglaze the pan with stock. Wash the poultry shears thoroughly and use them to cut it up.

BASICS ARE ON PP. 11–23 ... DON'T WALK AWAY ... CONCENTRATE ... FUCK THE GUESTS ... AND ALL THAT CONVIVALITY MALARKY ... DO NOT WASTE BREAD: OIL IT AND REBAKE IT ... STOCK! GET TREATMENT FOR SQUEAMISHNESS ... VEGETARIANISM IS CURABLE'

POULET À L'OIGNON /
CHICKEN AND ONIONS

This comes from my friend Jean-Pierre Xiradakis who serves it at La Tupiña in Bordeaux, a restaurant that has been rightly praised as 'paleolithic'. It is possibly the best restaurant in the world, certainly my favourite . . . Xiradakis got this dish from the writer and journalist Yves Harté who in turn got it from his mother who . . .

The recipe he gives in *La Cuisine de La Tupiña* proposes that for four people a chicken should be cut into eight pieces. I prefer to use four legs since they will all cook at the same rate. I also double the quantity of onions that he prescribes (think of soup the next day).

2KG SWEET ONIONS

4 CHICKEN LEGS

1 GLASS OF CHICKEN STOCK

(1 GLASS OF WHITE WINE – OPTIONAL)

(A FEW SCRAPS OF RAW HAM – OPTIONAL)

Slice the onions thinly. If your processor has the right kit use it. Whatever you do don't turn them to mush. Do NOT sweat them. Trust me. Brown the chicken legs in duck fat or olive oil. Put half the sliced onions in a high-sided pan with a lid. Add the chicken legs (and ham scraps). Put in the rest of the onions so that the legs are buried. Pour in stock (and wine). Season. Cook at 180°C for an hour.

As Xiradakis says, you will have scented the whole house.

Guinea fowl legs with stick celery is a spin-off worth investigating. Again, slice the celery thinly but don't blanch it. Do brown the legs.

BRAISED PHEASANT

15 STICKS CELERY

3 PHEASANTS

'SEASON . . . SALT . . . MAYBE PEPPER (CAN BE WHITE) . . . REMOVE THE GERM FROM GARLIC . . . COOK SPICES . . . BOIL OFF ALCOHOL . . . COOK TO PLEASE YOURSELF AS YOU MIGHT WRITE OR PAINT, DANCE OR SING TO PLEASE YOURSELF . . . CREATE YOUR OWN THEFTS . . .

100G PORK BACKFAT

100G BREADCRUMBS

1 EGG

STOCK

POWDERED CARAWAY

Cut the celery into 5cm pieces. Blanch them for 8 minutes.

Cut the breasts off the pheasants. Put them in hot butter so that they stiffen a bit and take some colour. Take the meat off the legs and the rest of the carcasses and mince it with the backfat and breadcrumbs; incorporate the beaten egg and a modest pinch of caraway. Shape in your hands to make squash-ball size boulettes.

Submerge the breasts in celery. Pour in 10cl stock. Put the boulettes on top of the celery. Put on to cook at a tremble for about an hour.

GIGOT DE LA CLINIQUE

The best-known recipe in the *Alice B. Toklas Cookbook* is for hashish fudge. She got the recipe from Brion Gysin who had got it in Tangier where it would have been known as *mahjoun*. It is of Berber origin. The problem with it is the problem of cannabis in any form – it turns the most delightful people into dull obsessives or insensate, giggling bores or borderline psychotics. Protracted exposure to the wretched stuff causes brain damage. Avoid. Stick to acid and opium.

The best recipe in the book is for a doubly marinated leg of lamb. It should serve 6 or maybe 8 people. This is from memory, my copy went missing years ago and I didn't bother to replace it.

The first marinade is conventional enough:

1 LEG OF LAMB

1 OR 2 BOTTLES OF DECENT RED WINE

OLIVE OIL

BASICS ARE ON PP. 11–23 ... DON'T WALK AWAY ... CONCENTRATE ... FUCK THE GUESTS ... AND ALL THAT CONVIVIALITY MALARKY ... DO NOT WASTE BREAD: OIL IT AND REBAKE IT ... STOCK! GET TREATMENT FOR SQUEAMISHNESS ... VEGETARIANISM IS CURABLE'

BAY LEAVES

JUNIPER BERRIES

PEPPERCORNS

CARAWAY SEEDS

A FEW CLOVES

This should cover the leg.

The second marinade is internal. You need a capacious syringe. A veterinary syringe is just the job. Fill it with a mixture of armagnac or cognac and orange juice – this last needs to be thoroughly filtered so that it doesn't block the needle. Shoot up the leg with about a wine glassful of the mixture every day for 10 days.

Salt the leg and roast for 60–80 mins at 200°C. Reduce the marinade.

The flavour is extraordinary. Gamey, savoury. It is habitually claimed to be akin to venison. Yet I have no taste for venison while I adore this meat's scented delicacy. Serve it with a potato purée.

In lieu of armagnac or cognac you could use mirabelle or kirsch or eau de vie de pomme or calvados or whisky or sake.

PARMENTIER

Shepherd's pie is an accredited health hazard in canteens, schools, hospitals. Hachis parmentier is different. Still, here is the one shepherd's pie recipe that is worth essaying. It was my father's. His genes and voice apart I have not nicked much from him so am unabashed about this theft.

LEFTOVER LAMB LEG OR SHOULDER

1KG ONIONS

CELERY

POTATO

MILK

BUTTER

GUINNESS

'SEASON ... SALT ... MAYBE PEPPER (CAN BE WHITE) ... REMOVE THE GERM FROM GARLIC ... COOK SPICES ... BOIL OFF ALCOHOL ... COOK TO PLEASE YOURSELF AS YOU MIGHT WRITE OR PAINT, DANCE OR SING TO PLEASE YOURSELF ... CREATE YOUR OWN THEFTS ...

WORCESTER SAUCE

ANGOSTURA BITTERS

Sweat 500g sliced onions and celery – cook till soft. Mince the meat. Mix meat and onions/celery with half a pint of Guinness, Worcester sauce and Angostura. Reduce till getting still liquid but going on sticky.

Mash potatoes with butter and milk. He liked them to be fairly stiff, and *to taste of potato.*

To the meat and veg add 500g sliced *uncooked* onions.

Place in an ovenproof dish and cover with mash. Dot with butter.

Cook at 150°C, no hotter, for an hour. He used to furrow it with a fork and finish it under the grill. I am not a fan of browned mashed potato.

My father's is a different dish from the various parmentiers that I habitually cook. These are modelled on the best I've tasted – Yves Camdeborde's when he was at La Régalade in furthest Montparnasse. He is a marvellous chef. His current restaurant, Le Comptoir du Relais, remains one of the hottest tickets in Paris. Extraordinarily, Parisians, of all people, are willing to queue at lunchtime when there is no booking. When we steal, we should steal from the finest.

The potato is a purée. Very definitely not mash. It is made with crème fraîche, a little garlic, a lot of unsalted butter, salt and pepper. (Beurre doux with salt added is some way away from salted butter.)

The purée does not sit on top of the filling, it surrounds it. So the buttered and oiled receptacle is lined with purée of about 3cm thickness and depth.

Here are some fillings: they are all more or less cooked and don't require long in the oven. Cook for about 25 minutes at 160°C.

Lamb's kidneys and liver. Chop small, partially cook and moisten with reduced stock before combining with the purée.

Black pudding/boudin noir. The addition of apples fried with cinnamon or of sweated onions is admissible, even advisable, depending on the components of the sausage. The best British black pudding comes from Stornoway (Charles Macleod or Macleod & Macleod) but, like Burgos morcilla, the amount of grain in them makes them perhaps too dry for this dish. The best French? There are too many contenders. Those that include chestnuts are worth avoiding. Those that include piment d'Espelette are to be sought. In general the softer, mousse-like texture of French boudins is the more appropriate in this instance. The boudin should be cut into 2–3 cm slices and mixed with the purée.

Duck confit. Take meat off the bone. Combine with chopped prunes, ideally from Agen, that have been soaked in sweet wine or vieille prune. Mix with purée.

Beef cheek (p. 95).

Chicken and mushroom. A nod here to chicken à la king, a fashionable dish of the late 1950s though apparently dating from the late 19th or early 20th century: there are of course numerous claimants to have been the original creator. They all claim equally that they have been plagiarised. Poach chicken breasts. Dice. Mix with button mushrooms and shallots cooked in butter till soft. Bind with crème fraîche. Particularly good for invalids with declining dental powers who are equally liable to be challenged by heavy spicing. So lay off all but comfort-spices: nutmeg, caraway, cumin. If used, use with moderation. If you use clove, watch out. Best don't.

BOEUF À LA FICELLE

1KG BEEF FILLET

STOCK

GREEN SAUCE (P. 29)

Beef on a string. The cooking method is primitive. The meat must be totally submerged; it has to be suspended in stock yet kept off the bottom of the pot. A wooden spoon that stretches across and exceeds the diameter of the

'SEASON . . . SALT . . . MAYBE PEPPER (CAN BE WHITE) . . . REMOVE THE GERM FROM GARLIC . . . COOK SPICES . . . BOIL OFF ALCOHOL . . . COOK TO PLEASE YOURSELF AS YOU MIGHT WRITE OR PAINT, DANCE OR SING TO PLEASE YOURSELF . . . CREATE YOUR OWN THEFTS . . .

pot is required. Attach the beef fillet with string to the spoon. Tie it round in 3 or 4 places. The stock must be boiling fiercely when the beef is lowered into it. And it must continue to boil fiercely. It will take 15–20 minutes.

Old restaurants that have been proposing the same menu for decades are the ones to go to: Kronenhalle in Zurich, Schiffergesellschaft in Lübeck, Plachutta in Vienna, Abel in Lyon, Barney Greengrass in New York. They are not sullied by innovation.

VITELLO TONNATO

This delicious, vaguely improbable and very simple dish is best done in quantity.

I thought it was well-known. A cosmopolitan bunch of guests – English, French, Turkish, Marseillais – recently disabused me of that proposition. None had even heard of it.

The questions you must ask are:

a) whether to roast the meat or simmer it and

b) whether to make a tuna sauce or a tuna mayonnaise.

The question I'm incapable of answering is where did I first eat it? No idea. As with many dishes the knowledge of it precedes the gustatory experience. And anticipation frequently precedes disappointment. That is unlikely to be the case here.

I know where I first read about it – in Elizabeth David's *Italian Food*. She gives two versions: see a) and b). Oh, the angst that comes with choice . . . *Silver Spoon*, Italian cooking's bible, opts to simmer. I too prefer to simmer the meat. Place it in a cold court-bouillon (p. 13) and bring to a very gentle murmur. Skim. Don't let the heat rise. Don't cook it to death.

BONED, THOROUGHLY TRIMMED VEAL RIB OR SHOULDER

COURT-BOUILLON OR VEAL STOCK

Sauce:

TINNED OR BOTTLED TUNA – HIGH-END STUFF

CAPERS IN VINEGAR

ANCHOVIES IN OIL

(HARD-BOILED EGG YOLKS – OPTIONAL)

SUNFLOWER OIL

OLIVE OIL

The sauce is made by processing the ingredients to form first a paste and then, with the addition of the sunflower oil and a modicum of olive oil, a smooth emulsion.

When the meat is done let it cool. Then slice it very thinly. Spread the sauce over it and add a few whole capers. Leave it for at least a few hours so that the veal takes on the sauce's flavour.

The neutral tones of the dish counter the preconception of Italian cooking as being excessively colourful. In the north pale is the norm: this is originally Piedmontese.

PORK BRAISED IN MILK

My cherished agent Anita Land and my great friend Jonathon Green are not going to be happy with this one.

Maiale al latte is double-treyf, an abomination to any Jew who is superstitious enough to put two-millennia-old proscriptions before gastronomic delight. Haven't we come on a bit since Exodus and Leviticus? These dismal rulebooks – all officiousness and menaces – that sought to stem the pursuit of pleasure should be binned. To judge by the proprietor of a restaurant in the former Roman ghetto round Portico d'Ottavia, Italian Jewry has an

'SEASON ... SALT ... MAYBE PEPPER (CAN BE WHITE) ... REMOVE THE GERM FROM GARLIC ... COOK SPICES ... BOIL OFF ALCOHOL ... COOK TO PLEASE YOURSELF AS YOU MIGHT WRITE OR PAINT, DANCE OR SING TO PLEASE YOURSELF ... CREATE YOUR OWN THEFTS ...

admirably relaxed attitude to dietary bullshit. When I asked this party why he prominently displayed a fat leg of cured ham on the bar, he looked at me with incredulous scorn and replied: 'Because we like it.' One imagines the Rabbanut, the supervising authority, has a practised blind eye and pretends to itself that the leg was formerly the property of that splendid animal which Israelis call 'king rabbit'.

I first ate this dish on its home territory at Alba in Piedmont one freezing lunchtime in December 1982. That is an appropriate month for it. The next day I had bagna cauda (p. 31), also previously untasted, in even worse climatic conditions.

IKG PORK FILLET OR LOIN IN ONE PIECE

IL MILK

200CL CREAM

OLIVE OIL

BUTTER

OPTIONAL: JUNIPER BERRIES, BAY LEAVES, LEMON ZEST,
CAPERS, GARLIC — WHOLE CLOVES, SLICED ONION,
CINNAMON, DRIED PORCINI, CHOPPED PANCETTA

Lightly brown the pork in butter and oil. Pour milk and cream over it and bring to near boil. Steady now. It must simmer at a murmur for 90 minutes or 2 hours. The milk will reduce, curdle (lemon zest and vinegary capers accelerate the process) and become granular. Don't worry. This dish is not a looker. But it tastes marvellous. The pork can be removed and the reduced milk put through a blender, though this is a merely cosmetic step.

The optional ingredients obviously flavour the milk and maybe the meat. I prefer to omit them.

It is, equally, a method that is applicable to veal: lessen the amount of milk and cream since a similarly sized piece of veal should not be cooked for more than an hour.

PORK FILLET WITH APPLES AND PRUNES

PORK FILLET

APPLES

PRUNES

STOCK

CALVADOS

CREAM

Brown the meat in butter (or duck fat). Peel and core the apples – use a variety that doesn't fall apart; the maligned Golden Delicious are fine. Quarter them. Brown them lightly in butter with piment d'Espelette or pimenton dulce. Put in an oiled/buttered gratin dish. Add a few diced pruneaux d'Agen. Moisten with a small glass of stock and small glass of calvados or vieille prune. Put the pork on top of them. Bake for 35 minutes at 200°C. Cover the pork with aluminium. Remove it to the bottom of the oven. Put 20cl of cream into the apples. When the cream has bubbled and reduced serve over the sliced meat.

STUFFED CABBAGE

This was one of the dishes cooked by Lotte Rigol, the second of the three young German women employed by my parents to look after me between the ages of three and seven. The smell from the kitchen was heavenly. Rather than Savoy cabbage she used white cabbage: perhaps that was all that was available in those days of rationing and shortages. Watching her tie it, tightly and intricately, was part of the pleasure. There was never any sauce save a glistening bouillon. One point of the dish was to make a little meat go a long way. Hence her inclusion of as much rice as meat. This version is less frugal but still hardly spendthrift. It combines what I can recall of Lotte's recipe with that which Pierre Koffmann gives in *Memories of Gascony*.

'SEASON . . . SALT . . . MAYBE PEPPER (CAN BE WHITE) . . . REMOVE THE GERM FROM GARLIC . . . COOK SPICES . . . BOIL OFF ALCOHOL . . . COOK TO PLEASE YOURSELF AS YOU MIGHT WRITE OR PAINT, DANCE OR SING TO PLEASE YOURSELF . . . CREATE YOUR OWN THEFTS . . .

SAVOY CABBAGE

400G FAT PORK

400G LEAN PORK

200G CHICKEN LIVERS

100G RAW HAM

250G BASMATI RICE

2 SHALLOTS

2 CLOVES GARLIC

STOCK

Cook the rice in stock. Process the fat pork, 200g of lean pork and the chicken livers till they are smooth. Process the remaining lean pork, the raw ham and the shallots and garlic coarsely, using the pulse button. Incorporate into the smooth mix. Add the cooked rice.

Cut out the hard core at the bottom of the cabbage and remove the tougher outer leaves. Blanch the cabbage for 10 minutes. Put it in iced water. Drain thoroughly. Now open it out like a large flower. Put a ball of meat mixture at the centre and fold leaves round it. Put more mix on the next layer of leaves and cover it. Continue until every layer of leaf is covered and the cabbage is more or less re-formed. Cut an ample length of string. Place the cabbage at the half-way mark and bind in every direction. When it is sufficiently secure not to release the stuffing, place it in a pot with stock about two-thirds of the way up it. Bring the stock to the boil and simmer for an hour under a lid. Be careful when snipping off the string not to let the thing collapse. Not that the flavour will be impaired.

MEATBALLS

Ray Liotta's character Henry Hill in *Goodfellas*: 'In prison, dinner was always a big thing. We had a pasta course, and then we had a meat or a fish. Paulie did the prep work. He was doing a year for contempt and had this wonderful system for doing the garlic. He used a razor, and he used to slice it so thin, it used to liquefy in the pan with just a little oil. It was a very good system'. It is only a very good system if the oil in the pan is at minimum heat. Garlic burns easily. The cooking in the film was done by Catherine Scorsese, mother of Martin, who also plays Joe Pesci's mother.

Her recipe for meatballs in tomato sauce with pasta can be found at **www.ew.com/article/1990/12/28/goodfellas-recipe** She advises:

a) Don't put in any oregano; it keeps repeating on you;

b) Don't fry the meatballs if they are to be cooked in the sauce.

I can't think of any circumstance in which I'd use oregano, a herb I dislike. Indeed I dislike most herbs. At the risk of provoking Mr Pesci's ire, I do fry the meatballs.

300G LEAN VEAL

300G LEAN PORK

300G LEAN BEEF

1 EGG

2 SHALLOTS

6 CLOVES GARLIC

OLIVE OIL

In a processor mince the shallots and garlic very finely. Add the meat and egg. Use the pulse button. The meat should not be ground to a pulp. It should be coarsely textured. Form into flattened ovaloid pieces – easier to get entirely brown. Fry in oil.

If you are going to do them with tomato sauce remove them when they are coloured and add to and simmer for an hour in Tomato sauce 1 (p. 26). If you are going to serve them as they are continue to fry for about 15 minutes.

'SEASON ... SALT ... MAYBE PEPPER (CAN BE WHITE) ... REMOVE THE GERM FROM GARLIC ... COOK SPICES ... BOIL OFF ALCOHOL ... COOK TO PLEASE YOURSELF AS YOU MIGHT WRITE OR PAINT, DANCE OR SING TO PLEASE YOURSELF ... CREATE YOUR OWN THEFTS ...

GARBURE

Infrequently encountered in restaurants, this is the lesser-known of south-west France's composed dishes. As with cassoulet there is no consensus about ingredients. Garbure can connote anything from a simple peasant soup to a festive peasant soup. The version here tends towards the latter: a French friend observed that it is too lavish to bear the name garbure. Once again it's a question of copying myself. I have been making garbures for a quarter of a century. But with a single exception I have never found one elsewhere that lives up to expectation. That one was made by a real master, Pierre Koffmann at La Tante Claire in Chelsea. Quite extraordinarily it was served with roast turbot; triumphantly served I might say . . .

END OF RAW HAM (TALON, TRÉBUC)

4 LEGS CONFIT DUCK

500G SALT PORK (NOT PETIT SALÉ WHICH IS TOO FAT)

4 TOULOUSE SAUSAGES

100G PORK RIND

2 CABBAGES

200G HARICOTS BLANCS

4 STICKS OF CELERY

2 CARROTS

2 ONIONS

2 LEEKS

2 SHALLOTS

4 TURNIPS

6 CLOVES GARLIC

STOCK

DUCK FAT

Soak the haricots blancs overnight. Cook them with the salt pork in ample water. When done cut the pork into chunks.

Cut the sausages into pieces of 6cm. Fry them till not quite done.

Sweat the onions, shallots and garlic.

Cut the cabbages into quarters. Remove the stems. Blanch in boiling water for 10 minutes.

Blanch the chopped up turnips.

Cut the raw ham and the pork rind into small pieces.

Put everything save the duck confit into a deep lidded pan. Add dilute stock and water to just about cover. Stir in a few spoonsful of duck fat.

Cook with the lid on for an hour at a low temperature. Add the confit. Cook for a further 15 minutes.

Serve with walnut oil and grilled bread rubbed with garlic.

Teaching himself to write, Robert Louis Stevenson *played the sedulous ape to Hazlitt, to Lamb, to Wordsworth, to Sir Thomas Browne . . .* The cook too must play the sedulous ape, imitating, wearing the clothes of his betters, trying on modes and mannerisms. But unlike the writer, unlike Stevenson whose imitative practices were to eventually produce in him the most limpid and beautiful prose, the cook must go no further than imitation. Art may concern itself with expression, a quality that has no role in craft.

LABSKAUS

Schiffergesellschaft in Lübeck is one of Europe's greatest restaurants. The beams of the former guildhall of that Hansa city's sea skippers are aptly hung with a beguilingly complex fleet of model ships. In the telly series *Magnetic North* we filmed Schiffergesellschaft's chef Gerhard Birnstingl making labskaus in, evidently, restaurant quantities. This recipe is guesswork based on watching him at work.

'SEASON . . . SALT . . . MAYBE PEPPER (CAN BE WHITE) . . . REMOVE THE GERM FROM GARLIC . . . COOK SPICES . . . BOIL OFF ALCOHOL . . . COOK TO PLEASE YOURSELF AS YOU MIGHT WRITE OR PAINT, DANCE OR SING TO PLEASE YOURSELF . . . CREATE YOUR OWN THEFTS . . .

Germany without potatoes is as unimaginable as a repeat offender suicide bomber. Labskaus, however, predates the introduction of the potato to Europe from South America in the 1500s. Till then the meat had been mixed with root vegetables. Not swede – which is actually Czech – but with rutabaga or turnip. Or with cereal – often in the form of crushed sea biscuit, hardtack. That was the version that was taken to Liverpool by visiting Baltic sailors or by returning Liverpudlian sailors. Liverpool transformed labskaus into something closer to Lancashire hotpot (and baeckeoffe). But the name hardly changed. It became naturalised as lobscouse. It was so widely eaten that the inhabitants of that independent city-state acquired its name. Whether willingly or mockingly, as a jibe, is moot. But scouse stuck. This instance of a people being called after what it supposedly eats (cf. rosbif, kiekefretter, kraut) is a vernacular form of metonymy.

2KG MASHED POTATOES

1KG SALT BEEF, CHOPPED

2 BAKED, PEELED BEETROOTS (THAT HAVE NEVER SNIFFED VINEGAR)

6 NEW GREEN CUCUMBERS

Put all the ingredients through a food mill. The colour and texture will be alarming. Magenta slurry. Don't worry. It tastes marvellous. More than marvellous with the addition of a fried egg or two and a matjes fillet.

LANCASHIRE HOTPOT

Stolen word for word from Anthony Burgess (whose shade does not disapprove). 'It needs very slow cooking in an oven. Into a family-sized, brown, oval-shaped dish with a lid, you place the following ingredients: best end of neck of lamb, trimmed of all fat; potatoes and onions thickly sliced. These go in alternate layers. Season well, cover with good stock, top with oysters or, if you wish, sliced beef kidneys. There is no need for officious timing: you will know when it is done. Serve with pickled red cabbage and a cheap

claret. In his novel *The Human Factor*, Mr Graham Greene has the effrontery to add carrots to the dish. He promised to remove those carrots in a
re-issue of the book, but they are still redly and wrongly there.'

BAECKEOFFE

Another dish that was 'traditionally' cooked in a baker's oven. This folksy
provenance belongs to the same orthodoxy as every French chef having the
obligatory stove-slave grandmother who made exquisite yet authentically
downhome dishes from the pike and pigeon that grandfather hunter-
gathered morning to dusk when he wasn't dispensing cracker-barrel wisdom
and mainlining calvados.

It is important to use potatoes that won't fall apart and turn the thing
to mush.

IKG WAXY POTATOES

500G BEEF BRISKET

500G PORK HAND

500G LAMB SHOULDER

2 PIG'S TROTTERS

500G ONIONS

250G CARROTS

4 CLOVES GARLIC

Marinade:

20CL GIN

75CL RIESLING

JUNIPER BERRIES

2 BAY LEAVES

3 CLOVES

'SEASON ... SALT ... MAYBE PEPPER (CAN BE WHITE) ... REMOVE THE GERM FROM GARLIC
... COOK SPICES ... BOIL OFF ALCOHOL ... COOK TO PLEASE YOURSELF AS YOU MIGHT
WRITE OR PAINT, DANCE OR SING TO PLEASE YOURSELF ... CREATE YOUR OWN THEFTS ...

Cut the meats into pieces about 4cm by 4cm. Marinate for at least 24 hours in the riesling, juniper berries, bay leaves and cloves. Peel and slice the potatoes, onions and carrots thinly. Strain the marinade. Put a layer of potatoes in the pot, a layer of onions and carrots, a layer of meat with the trotters, a further layer of potatoes and so on. Pour on the strained marinade. If the pot's lid is not tight make a flour and water paste to secure it. Cook for 5 hours at 120°C.

A chauvinistic French boast: what do you call really good German cooking? You call it Alsacien cooking. That is to claim Alsace as France, which it is, at the moment – *de jure*. The actuality is more complicated, characteristic of many border provinces, disputed territories where nationality is a fluid construct, where loyalty and identity are more than usually regional. The more a people is preoccupied with identity the more tenaciously it clings to emblems of permanence, of its chosen past – among them particular dishes.

Like, say, religion as a way of life, this is undoubtedly puzzling to the English whose attitude towards their heritage – gastronomic as well as architectural – is one of shrugging indifference, carelessness, negligence; there is much to be said for sloth. These qualities are hardly laudable but they are less toxic, less closed than the boastful specialness that accompanies pride in identity, in race, in endogamy, in a culture whose limits are defined. An English plagiarist, not weighed down by the burden of belonging, can steal from anywhere: his oyster is indeed pan-global. An Alsacien plagiarist must confine himself to thefts from within the tribe, to within the prescribed boundaries, thus to Alsace, Strasbourg and the lands that stretch inexorably east from the right bank of the Rhine to the Oder and beyond: a central European oyster. A hungry revenant from 1871, when Alsace was annexed by Bismarck, would have no difficulty in recognising the city's culinary repertoire, which is exemplary in its conservatism. While the rest of France is susceptible to fashion and crazes, coulis and foams, Alsace is doggedly wedded to being Alsace, the province where mittel Europe ends and culinary invention never begins. It is always the same. I love it.

BASICS ARE ON PP. 11–23 . . . DON'T WALK AWAY . . . CONCENTRATE . . . FUCK THE GUESTS . . . AND ALL THAT CONVIVIALITY MALARKY . . . DO NOT WASTE BREAD: OIL IT AND REBAKE IT . . . STOCK! GET TREATMENT FOR SQUEAMISHNESS . . . VEGETARIANISM IS CURABLE'

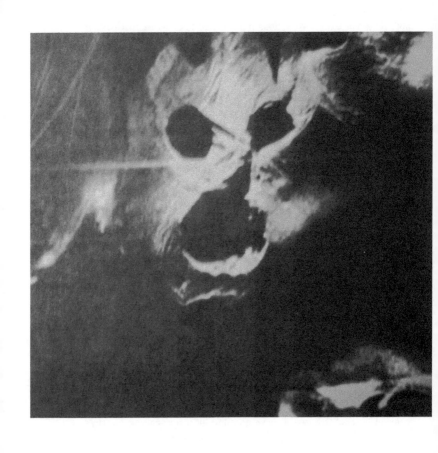

HARE: THE ONLY WAY

I have a problem here. Since childhood hare has been my favourite game, a taste I share with F. X. Enderby who breakfasted off reheated hare stew with pickled walnuts; the hare being a gift from 'arry, near toothless chef at The Conway, whose preference was for 'red coorant jelly and an 'art shaped croutong'.

I loved watching them, pre-game, on the downs at the eastern escarpment of Cranborne Chase above the Avon valley and close by two mysterious sites, Great Yews and Vanity, the former self-evident and magnificent, the latter the hardly discernible ruins of a house so called where blackthorn bushes grew in abundance and shone iridescent with sloes in late summer.

I loved eating hares. As I have mentioned elsewhere my father used often to have a .22 in the car and would shoot them if they were lolloping within range. He had polished cigarette holders which he had made from hare bones . . . I found these creepy, though less creepy than Himmler's furniture made from human bones which I read about, shivering.

Then, many years after my father's death, for the only time ever, never to be repeated, I moved to the country, north of Bordeaux. This is when Levi the Leveret came into our life: he wasn't exactly a pet, rather a familiar who trusted us, sunbathed within a few metres of the house, hid under shrubs. Which is hardly surprising given that every weekend during the miraculously elastic 'season' the French countryside is alive with shooters in day-glo citrus-coloured jackets. No matter that the high-viz kit may be as highly visible as the Alps it does not prevent an annual autumnal cull of doughty combine-harvester drivers and gung-ho loggers. My condolences to their families. But what concerned me was Levi's wellbeing and, eventually, that of his fellow prey. Stricken by sentimental irreason and gross self-indulgence I resolved that I would never again eat hare. Not that hares are capable of conning my sacrifice. Not that the high-viz battalions will take a blind bit of notice. Nor, I trust, will my readers pay any attention to this appeasement of my grubby conscience.

This is the recipe I have adapted from that which my mother used. It includes sloe gin which is hardly canonical but apt given the proximity of hares to the place where I used to gather sloes.

HARE, JOINTED

HARE OFFAL AND BLOOD

CHOCOLATE

SULTANAS

PRUNES

Marinade:

150CL RED WINE

20CL RED WINE VINEGAR

20CL SLOE GIN

JUNIPER BERRIES

PEPPERCORNS

DRIED ORANGE PEEL

BAY LEAVES

GARLIC

ONION STUCK WITH CLOVES

PORK RIND

Marinate the hare for several days. Remove from marinade. Dry and brown in duck fat.

Strain the marinade. Put it and the hare into a vessel with a tight lid. Add a couple of squares of bitter chocolate, some sultanas and prunes, and the minced liver, heart and kidneys. Cook in a very low oven for 4 hours till the meat is falling off the bone. Remove the hare and keep warm. Reduce the sauce if necessary. If you have the hare's blood (which should be kept in the fridge with some vinegar) add it to the reduced sauce but don't let it boil – if you do so the blood will curdle.

Serve with buttered noodles and guilt.

'SEASON . . . SALT . . . MAYBE PEPPER (CAN BE WHITE) . . . REMOVE THE GERM FROM GARLIC . . . COOK SPICES . . . BOIL OFF ALCOHOL . . . COOK TO PLEASE YOURSELF AS YOU MIGHT WRITE OR PAINT, DANCE OR SING TO PLEASE YOURSELF . . . CREATE YOUR OWN THEFTS . . .

SHEFTALIA

When Charlotte Street and Camden Town were gastronomically Cypriot, virtually every café and restaurant offered sheftalia. The best of those places – Koritsas and Nontas – are long gone and the few that remain hawk meat patties without caul fat though they retain the name, fraudulently.

750G PORK SHOULDER OR 500G LEAN PORK AND 250G PORK
    BACK FAT

CAUL FAT

SWEET ONION

PARSLEY

PEPPER

Mince the meat so that the back fat is spread throughout the mixture. Add raw chopped onion, chopped parsley and ground pepper. Form the meat into a large blob.

Submerge the caul fat in acidulated water. Dry it. Cut into pieces sufficient to wrap round pieces of meat mixture 8cm × 3cm.

Ideally they should be cooked on a barbecue. A very hot grill will do. They'll need 20 minutes, turned after 10.

CASSOULET

This is one of the world's great dishes. It should be approached with seriousness. But not with undue reverence. There is no true way. There is no definitive inventory of ingredients. There is no immutable method. There are schools and schisms and bickering factions, often within the same cook. My ideas have changed over the years, largely because indisputably the best cassoulet I have eaten was indisputably incorrect; that is, incorrect according to the prescription I had then long adhered to.

In the mid-Nineties I drove for more than a week round the cassoulet belt of south-west France in an attempt to find the cassoulet that defined cassoulet. The one. This was a daft idea that turned out to be a dismal failure. Version after version lurched between mediocre and moderate. Many of the guilty parties were big name restaurants. This wasn't like Marseille where bouillabaisse turns out to be an occitan word for 'we seen you coming'. There was no scam involved, just repeatedly torpid, tired, approximate cooking.

Nothing began to approach even the foothills of the cassoulet at Alain Dutournier's Au Trou Gascon, 700km north in the 12th arrondissement of Paris, near Omnisport Bercy. If there's a lesson here it is that best is not to be found on home territory. And if there's a second lesson it is that our prejudices are there to be broken down so that we can begin to build a replacement set based in our empirical observations.

Lamb! Dutournier's recipe includes lamb. And tomato. And carrot. Heresies, all of them. The second time I went to Au Trou Gascon Dutournier had installed his former sous-chef Jacques Faussat and had himself moved on to his swankier Carré des Feuillants. Faussat was as good as his master. I must have eaten his cassoulet three or four times. Then one lunchtime I ordered it and, well, there was something different about it. The parts were there, the whole wasn't. Yes, the recipe seemed to be the same . . . but cooking is about more than recipes. Even though I knew the answer I asked a waiter:

Is M Faussat no longer here?

He has moved on.

That's a shame.

No, no. Now we have M Godiard.

Evidently.

I still advise against tomato and carrot, on grounds of colour as much as anything, but am won round to lamb, just so long as Dutournier or Faussat (whose own restaurant La Braisière is in the 17th arrondissement) is cooking. Another self-imposed rule is no smoked meat.

It is a dish that should be cooked in large quantities. This recipe is for about 12 people. Or, if you happen to be Robin Yapp or Alain Juppé, half that number.

In the autumn of 1996 we walked into the Auberge Pyrénées Cévennes in rue de la Folie-Méricourt only to be looked up and down by three guys in loden coats. But though their garb was BCBG, the guys weren't and though they were at the bar they were merely pretending to drink.

'SEASON . . . SALT . . . MAYBE PEPPER (CAN BE WHITE) . . . REMOVE THE GERM FROM GARLIC . . . COOK SPICES . . . BOIL OFF ALCOHOL . . . COOK TO PLEASE YOURSELF AS YOU MIGHT WRITE OR PAINT, DANCE OR SING TO PLEASE YOURSELF . . . CREATE YOUR OWN THEFTS . . .

We had no sooner sat down than there was a rush of urgency by the door. In hurried Alain Juppé, prime minister and some years off taking the rap for Chirac (punishment: exile to Quebec), hurling his loden at an aide. Juppé is a lean man, and was he hungry . . . The three guards and a further two who had swifted in with him went into deep conversation for 30 seconds whereupon they were served with what can only be described as a sinkful of cassoulet, a vessel 1m × 0.75m, and deep. Their demolition of it was amazingly swift, neat, brutal – as though taking out some Sunni botherer.

Three years earlier my mother had died. The weeks of arranging the funeral, sorting through her house and dealing with death's bureaucracy were predictably dismal. My bored gloom was relieved by a phone call from the only wine merchant in Britain to have received V. S. Naipaul's imprimatur, Robin Yapp. He suggested that I come to lunch. What a lunch! Robin and Judith were well acquainted with my fondness for cassoulet and had with great generosity confected one to console me. World class? Nah – this was different class (which is classier than world class). The sheer volume was daunting but we were not in the mood to be daunted.

1.5KG HARICOT BEANS – TARBES, ARPAJON AND SOISSONS
   ARE THE MOST ESTEEMED

PORK RIND

2 ONIONS STUCK WITH CLOVES

1 HEAD OF GARLIC

500G SALT PORK – NOT BELLY, A LEANER CUT

1 END OF RAW HAM ON THE BONE

250G DICED RAW HAM

1 LARGE GARLIC BOILING SAUSAGE

Soak the beans overnight. Bring to the boil in plenty of water. Discard the water. Bring to a simmer in fresh water with the other ingredients. Skim. Cook for 90 minutes. Discard the pork rinds, onion and garlic. Do NOT discard the liquid. Chop the meats into 4cm × 4cm dice.

BASICS ARE ON PP. 11–23 . . . DON'T WALK AWAY . . . CONCENTRATE . . . FUCK THE GUESTS . . . AND ALL THAT CONVIVIALITY MALARKY . . . DO NOT WASTE BREAD: OIL IT AND REBAKE IT . . . STOCK! GET TREATMENT FOR SQUEAMISHNESS . . . VEGETARIANISM IS CURABLE'

8 TOULOUSE SAUSAGES OR ITALIAN ALL PORK SAUSAGES,
QUARTERED

IKG PORK LOIN, CHOPPED 4CM DICE

(IF YOU ARE GOING TO INCLUDE LAMB REDUCE THE PORK
TO 500G AND ADD THE SAME AMOUNT OF CUBED LAMB
SHOULDER)

4 ONIONS, SLICED

Roast the chopped pork loin (and lamb) and the quartered sausages in duck fat for 10 minutes at 150°C. Add the onions and cook for a further 10 minutes so they soften but don't brown.

PORK RIND

2L STOCK

IO CLOVES GARLIC

8 CONFIT LEGS OF DUCK (TAKE OFF THE BONE)

BREADCRUMBS

Assemble everything. Put pork rinds on the bottom of the vessel. Then a layer of beans, a layer of boiled meats, more beans, roasted meat/sausages, more rinds (which add to the unctuousness), garlic, beans, confit and so on. Distribute the ingredients evenly. Add the beans' cooking liquid and stock. A cassoulet should be quite liquid. Sprinkle the top with breadcrumbs. Spray with duck fat. Cook at a low heat, 130°C, for 2 hours. Watch it. Top up with stock if necessary. The folksy practice of breaking the crust 7 times and pushing it down into the cassoulet is inadvisable because it over-thickens the liquid.

What I often do nowadays when I have to, say, describe a room, is to take a page of a dictionary, any page at all, and see if with the words suggested by that one page in the dictionary I can build up a room, build up a scene . . . I even did it in a novel I wrote called MF. *There's a description of a hotel vestibule*

'SEASON . . . SALT . . . MAYBE PEPPER (CAN BE WHITE) . . . REMOVE THE GERM FROM GARLIC . . . COOK SPICES . . . BOIL OFF ALCOHOL . . . COOK TO PLEASE YOURSELF AS YOU MIGHT WRITE OR PAINT, DANCE OR SING TO PLEASE YOURSELF . . . CREATE YOUR OWN THEFTS . . .

*whose properties are derived from Page 167 in R. J. Wilkinson's
Malay-English dictionary. Nobody has noticed . . . As most
things in life are arbitrary anyway, you're not doing anything
naughty, you're really normally doing what nature does, you're
just making an entity out of the elements. I do recommend it
to young writers.* Anthony Burgess, *Writer's Digest*, 1975,
vol. 55, No. 8, page 13.

GAME TIMBALE

This derives at several removes from sartu, devised for Naples' Bourbon
rulers by their local chefs the *monzus* (an approximation of monsieur which
is also perhaps the source of that delightful form of address 'Mush!'). The
dish, too, is an approximation, an Italian rendering of French taste or a
second-guessing of absolutist taste. Either way it is a bizarre hybrid and
the very epitome of maximalist cooking; its recipe is an inventory, there are
dozens of conflicting ingredients. Its genesis has some correspondence to
that of vincisgrassi.

There is a photograph of the dish, of which I was previously ignorant, in
Silver Spoon (the omniscient Italian equivalent of *Larousse Gastronomique*):
my ignorance was odd for a sartu recipe is included in Elizabeth David's
Italian Food, a now ailing copy of which I've owned most of my adult life;
still, no one reads a cookbook cover to cover. The sliced sartu looked so
seductive that I didn't bother to read the recipe that accompanied it. I simply
nicked the basic idea: a pie whose crust is rice. A real sartu is, evidently, not
a dish to be undertaken lightly. It requires several hours' preparation. The
sheer labour involved is detailed in a blog by the gastronomically obsessed
Neapolitan hairstylist Giuseppe Topo, a personable-sounding fellow whose
'what are you going to eat on your holiday' is a step up from the usual
enquiry.

This timbale (sartu is a name peculiar to Naples) is less demanding but
still not one for the shirker.

BASICS ARE ON PP. 11–23 . . . DON'T WALK AWAY . . . CONCENTRATE . . . FUCK THE GUESTS . . . AND
ALL THAT CONVIVIALITY MALARKY . . . DO NOT WASTE BREAD: OIL IT AND REBAKE
IT . . . STOCK! GET TREATMENT FOR SQUEAMISHNESS . . . VEGETARIANISM IS CURABLE'

The filling is a sort of salmi.

BASIC RISOTTO (P. 141)

2 EGG YOLKS

BUTTER

FINE BREADCRUMBS

Salmi:

STOCK

2 PHEASANTS

2 PIGEONS

2 ONIONS

2 CARROTS

40CL MARSALA

75CL RED WINE

CLOVES

JUNIPER BERRIES

PEPPERCORNS

DRIED ORANGE PEEL

DRIED CEPS

CHOCOLATE

Reduce the wines by half with the aromatics, peel, chocolate.

Roast the birds, onions, carrots for 15 minutes at 220°C.

Take the meat off the carcasses. Add the meat, veg, juices from the deglazed pan and the carcasses to the reduced wine. Top up with stock. Simmer for 15 minutes.

Take the meat out of the sauce and chop into sensible-sized pieces. Strain the sauce. Reduce it till it is beginning to get sticky. Return the meat to it.

Generously butter a soufflé dish (or similar). Spread a decent coat of fine breadcrumbs over the buttered surfaces. Incorporate the egg yolks into the

'SEASON . . . SALT . . . MAYBE PEPPER (CAN BE WHITE) . . . REMOVE THE GERM FROM GARLIC . . . COOK SPICES . . . BOIL OFF ALCOHOL . . . COOK TO PLEASE YOURSELF AS YOU MIGHT WRITE OR PAINT, DANCE OR SING TO PLEASE YOURSELF . . . CREATE YOUR OWN THEFTS . . .

risotto. Line the dish with the risotto: about 2cm deep for the sides, 3cm for the bottom. You have a well. Fill it with the meat. (Do this tentatively. If the sauce appears to be too runny put it back on a gentle heat to reduce it further. When a satisfactory texture is achieved proceed.) Put a layer of risotto across the top of the well. Add a dusting of breadcrumbs.

Bake for 30 minutes at 220°C. Unmould it on to a large plate. It looks spectacular. But if it proves disobliging don't worry. The unmoulding is, after all, only for appearance's sake and this is a book that eats with its tongue rather than its eyes. Having said that, I must admit to a chromatic bias. The intense wine-darkness of a salmi served *tel quel* appeals less to me than the pale tan of breadcrumbed rice which occludes that intensity.

BEEF CHEEK

1KG BEEF CHEEK

1KG ONIONS

8 CLOVES GARLIC

4 BAY LEAVES

8 JUNIPER BERRIES, CRUSHED

1 SMALL SPOON OF PIMENTON PICCANTE

1 SMALL SPOON OF PIMENTON DULCE

BLACK PEPPER

PINCH OF GRATED NUTMEG

PINCH OF POWDERED CLOVE

1 SQUARE BITTER CHOCOLATE

4 PIECES DRIED ORANGE PEEL

4 ANCHOVIES

1 BOTTLE OF PORT

STOCK

OLIVE OIL

CUP OF STRONG ESPRESSO

BASICS ARE ON PP. 11–23 ... DON'T WALK AWAY ... CONCENTRATE ... FUCK THE GUESTS ... AND ALL THAT CONVIVIALITY MALARKY ... DO NOT WASTE BREAD: OIL IT AND REBAKE IT ... STOCK! GET TREATMENT FOR SQUEAMISHNESS ... VEGETARIANISM IS CURABLE'

Sweat the onions and garlic with the pimenton and spices for 40 minutes on a low heat in oil till they are melted. A pan with a tight-fitting lid is required.

In another pan brown the beef. Not cut up.

Pour the port into the onions and bring to the boil for a couple of minutes. Turn down to a tremble. Put in the beef, chocolate, peel, coffee (don't be scared) and anchovies. Cover with stock.

Cook it in a low oven (130°C) for 4 hours.

LA SAUCE

The Merrie Englander Cecil Sharp collected folksongs, mostly in Somerset and the Appalachians. Quite how folky these folksongs are is moot. David Harker, Sharp's sternest critic, believes that the majority derive from 'broadsides', simple songsheets, and that 'the oral tradition' is chimerical. It is indisputable that someone created these songs, whether as broadsides or in some other form. They do not appear out of the blue. (Anon) was a person.

Sharp was almost certainly sold pups. He heard what he wanted to hear. And the denizens of the pubs and taprooms that were his laboratories soon learned what he wanted to hear. They duly obliged him: in return for another pint, for another plug of baccy, they improvised amended versions of extant songs and maybe, *pace* David Harker, made up new songs in their cups. It has been known.

In the greatest self-portrait of the 20th century Christian Schad wears a diaphanous green blouse and an expression of blank *je m'en foutisme*. He stands in front of a woman naked save for a red stocking and a wrist ribbon. She has a scar on her face. The Tate Gallery owns this sublime work. Its tasting note instructs us that the scar on the woman's cheek is a *freggio* (sic), a sort of brand, particular to Naples, inflicted by her boyfriend or keeper to make her 'unattractive to others. It is a startling emblem of the potential violence underlying male possession of the female body'. This is as dubious as it gets. It might be a *warning* to others to keep away. And to supply the detached painter with a right-on, early 21st century, quasi-feminist purpose

'SEASON ... SALT ... MAYBE PEPPER (CAN BE WHITE) ... REMOVE THE GERM FROM GARLIC ... COOK SPICES ... BOIL OFF ALCOHOL ... COOK TO PLEASE YOURSELF AS YOU MIGHT WRITE OR PAINT, DANCE OR SING TO PLEASE YOURSELF ... CREATE YOUR OWN THEFTS ...

is absurd. But this is the Tate – and the *freggio* is otherwise unknown. The only references to it derive from this note. The word *fregio* – one g – is the first person singular of *fregiare*, to embellish or ornament, especially with a frieze. Its use in this specialised sense is sui generis, without detectable precursors. There are 19th-century photographs of women so scarred. But by the time Schad came to Naples in 1920 the practice had been abandoned. It belonged to a gruesome lower depths folklore which evidently appealed to him and which would, in the way of such urban mythology, have been routinely exaggerated. The word for this sort of scar was *sfregio*. Schad had little Italian. The artists of the Neue Sachlichkeit weren't *sachlichkeit*, they weren't 'objective'. It is a misleading handle, the coinage of a typically taxonomically inclined art historian G. F. Hartlaub. Schad's paintings were inventions. It is probable that the *freggio*, the misheard or mistranscribed *sfregio*, was equally his invention.

Elizabeth David was as much a folklorist as a cook. Her work, like that of her contemporary Jane Grigson, weathers fashion's vicissitudes not because of its culinary utility but because of the quality of the prose, the ethnographic inquisitiveness and ultimately the pleasure that is to be derived from a lucid presence.

The recipe for la Sauce au Vin du Medoc was passed on to her by an oenologist, Patricia Green, on behalf of one Madame Bernard, wife of a viticulteur at Cissac-Medoc, north-west of Pauillac. It appears in *French Provincial Cooking*. And that's it. It is nowhere else to be found.

This was puzzling. I asked Jean-Pierre Xiradakis (p. 70), as much a collector of recipes as Mrs David, if he had heard of it. No. He in turn asked the historian Philippe Méyzie who has written widely on Girondin cooking and is as encyclopaedic as Xiradakis. No. Further, it goes unmentioned in Alcide Bontou's *Traité de cuisine bourgeoise bordelais* (1898), which does not restrict itself to the bourgeois table.

Did it have any existence prior to *French Provincial Cooking*? It is improbable that Mrs David emulated Schad's deadpan cunning and invented it. But it is altogether possible that Madame Bernard, apprised of a patrician English recipe-collector prowling the vinous peninsula, made up a dish of such extravagance that it would prove irresistible to her: she does indeed refer to it as a 'collector's piece'. If she was had, she was had with a smile.

Whatever its provenance, or lack of provenance, it is a fine dish. The method, if that's the word, is the same whatever the components.

1 RABBIT

1 HARE

2KG BEEF BRISKET OR SILVERSIDE

1KG LEAN PORK

500G CARROTS

ONIONS

SHALLOTS

GARLIC

BAY LEAVES

2 BOTTLES OF A RED WINE HEAVIER THAN A MEDOC

75CL WATER

CHOCOLATE

CUP OF STRONG ESPRESSO

Joint the rabbit, and hare (if you must – p. 87). Brown them and the other meats cut into large chunks. Sweat the onions, shallots and garlic. Put all ingredients together. Pour on wine, bring to boil. Lower heat, simmer gently for 4 or 5 hours at 120°C. Leave to get cold. Reheat the next day for a couple of hours. Serve with potato purée.

This dish is colloquially known as Car Crash'n'Smash. Batchelors' Smash is a form of instant mashed potato, fairly disgusting, a long-lived relic of the 1960s. Convenience foods characterised that decade more than Mrs David did. The Stones were on the money, 'Cooking fresh food for a husband's such a drag'.

TAFELSPITZ

BEEF TOPSIDE

ONIONS, CARROTS, CELERIAC, LEEK

'SEASON . . . SALT . . . MAYBE PEPPER (CAN BE WHITE) . . . REMOVE THE GERM FROM GARLIC . . . COOK SPICES . . . BOIL OFF ALCOHOL . . . COOK TO PLEASE YOURSELF AS YOU MIGHT WRITE OR PAINT, DANCE OR SING TO PLEASE YOURSELF . . . CREATE YOUR OWN THEFTS . . .

PEPPERCORNS

STOCK

HORSERADISH ROOT

CREAM

Viennese butchery is more precise than British. Still, the British cut, topside, is a near analogue of that served at Plachutta, a restaurant that has been around forever. Each serving should be a slice of topside about 3–4cm thick.

Brown halved unskinned onions without oil. Add the meat and stock. Simmer it for 120 minutes. Skim now and again. Add carrots, celeriac, leeks, peppercorns. Make a sauce by combining grated horseradish and cream. Usually accompanied by bratkartoffeln (p. 121) and apple sauce – iffy, censored.

POT AU FEU

A crock of folklore and some very bogus science is attached to this dish. Ignore.

The cooking times of the meats vary considerably. However the meats reheat at about the same rate. And it gains from reheating. So cook the meats separately one day and assemble them together the next.

6 CARROTS

6 FENNEL BULBS

6 TURNIPS

2 CELERIAC

6 LEEKS

I CABBAGE

12 ONIONS

12 CLOVES GARLIC

750G BEEF BRISKET

750G BEEF SHANK

I DUCK

1 CHICKEN – A BOILING CHICKEN IF AVAILABLE

6 MARROWBONES, SPLIT LENGTHWAYS

JUNIPER BERRIES

BAY LEAVES

STOCK

Simmer the carrots, fennel, celeriac, turnips. Later add the leeks, which take less time to cook.

Blanch the cabbage and simmer by itself.

A great deal of stock is required. All the meats must be submerged. All pots must be skimmed regularly.

Put the beef with half the onions, garlic and aromatics in stock and simmer for 3–4 hours.

Divide the rest of the garlic, onions, etc. between the chicken and the duck.

A boiling chicken (not a broiler) will need at least 2 hours in stock, which it will enrich immeasurably. A roasting chicken will take 50–60 minutes.

A duck will cook within 60–70 minutes, again in stock.

Allow all ingredients to cool when they have cooked and remove them from the cooking liquids. Refrigerate overnight. Remove the fat from the meat stock.

Reheat everything together in the meat stock. Do it gently. Add vegetable stock if needed. Roast the marrowbones in a very hot oven. Scrape out the marrow and add it to the broth.

My preference is to serve the broth, vegetables and meat together in soup plates rather than as two separate courses.

Serve with Tomato sauce 1 (p. 26) or Green sauce (p. 29) or Aillade (p. 33) or horseradish cream. Not too much of any of them.

JAMBON BEURRE

Hardly surprisingly, Jacques Brel's favourite dish was mussels and chips. However, he once claimed that the single best meal of his life was a ham

'SEASON ... SALT ... MAYBE PEPPER (CAN BE WHITE) ... REMOVE THE GERM FROM GARLIC ... COOK SPICES ... BOIL OFF ALCOHOL ... COOK TO PLEASE YOURSELF AS YOU MIGHT WRITE OR PAINT, DANCE OR SING TO PLEASE YOURSELF ... CREATE YOUR OWN THEFTS ...

sandwich he ate on the train from Paris back to Brussels; he had just secured a recording contract. The quality of SNCF ham sandwiches then, in 1953, was probably higher than it would become. Not of course that *what* he was eating prompted his superlative. There's more to it than that.

Today after many years of industrial abuse (approximate meat, kapok bread) and competition from such imports as burgers, tacos, doners and wraps, France has discovered that the '*legendaire . . . mythique*' (not my words) jambon beurre is the *ne plus ultra* of 'le street food' (again . . .).

> BREAD
>
> HAM
>
> BUTTER
>
> MUSTARD

Halve a good fresh baguette, one that is crisp without and honeycombed within. Cut it along its length but stop short of completely separating the two pieces. Smother one surface in unsalted butter, the other in Dijon mustard. Between them shove several slices of highest quality cooked ham, the kind that tastes of pig rather than of factory floor.

> There is something aberrant about restaurateurs and chefs who offer – and I am not making this up – waffle crusted chicken bites, maple syrup floss, cola chilli drizzle, salted air foam(!?), micro coriander and gruyer (sic) cheese. Pity the poor fools. They need help. Or a gig in Dubai.

BASICS ARE ON PP. 11–23 . . . DON'T WALK AWAY . . . CONCENTRATE . . . FUCK THE GUESTS . . . AND ALL THAT CONVIVALITY MALARKY . . . DO NOT WASTE BREAD: OIL IT AND REBAKE IT . . . STOCK! GET TREATMENT FOR SQUEAMISHNESS . . . VEGETARIANISM IS CURABLE'

OFFAL

VEAL KIDNEY WITH MUSTARD

I VEAL KIDNEY

125G BUTTON MUSHROOMS/CHAMPIGNONS DE PARIS

2 SHALLOTS

40CL CREAM

15CL WHITE PINEAU DE CHARENTES

15CL REDUCED STOCK

DIJON MUSTARD

Cook button mushrooms and shallots, both thinly sliced, in butter till they are just beginning to soften and colour. Pour in 20cl cream. Keep them just about bubbling. Slice the kidneys into mini chunks. Fry them in oil, stirring. Put them in a colander to drain. Deglaze the pan with pineau de Charentes. Add the mushrooms and shallots, a further 20cl of cream, the reduced stock and the mustard (as much as you judge necessary). Reintroduce the kidneys to heat through.

BASICS ARE ON PP. 11–23 ... DON'T WALK AWAY ... CONCENTRATE ... FUCK THE GUESTS ... AND ALL THAT CONVIVALITY MALARKY ... DO NOT WASTE BREAD: OIL IT AND REBAKE IT ... STOCK! GET TREATMENT FOR SQUEAMISHNESS ... VEGETARIANISM IS CURABLE'

TRIPE AND ONIONS

Cuisine gran'mère. Literally. *My* actual grandmother, Agnes Hogg, my mother's mother, used, fag in mouth, to prepare this for Saturday lunch when, every other weekend, my mother and I would make the half-hour train journey from Salisbury to Southampton: West Dean, Lockerley, Dunbridge, Romsey, So'ton Central . . . the route excited me, part of it was that of the abandoned Southampton to Salisbury canal. But there never was a station at Lockerley and West Dean was merely Dean. Still, it was a long time ago. Such a long time that till recently I had forgotten the jungle lushness of the surrounding country.

My memory of those lunches is surer. Grandma's version was richer, creamier and less soupy than that which my mother herself cooked. I guess that she thickened the sauce with flour, and just a hint of Kensitas ash.

1.5KG WASHED TRIPE, CUT INTO CIGARETTE SIZE STRIPS

750G ONIONS SLICED THINLY

1L MILK

500CL CREAM

NUTMEG

WHITE PEPPER

Put the lot, apart from the cream, into a double boiler and bring just to the boil. Simmer for 90 minutes. Check frequently – overdone tripe turns to mushy elastic. Add the cream after about 70 minutes. The tripe should be al dente, the milk and cream much reduced. Serve it with potato purée.

TRIPE WITH BEER

Le Bistrot Lillois, 40 rue de Gand, Lille. I ate a fine tripes à la bière followed by pain perdu. The chef, M Dewailly, was standing beaming outside as I left. I congratulated him on a delicious meal. I asked: how do you do the

'SEASON . . . SALT . . . MAYBE PEPPER (CAN BE WHITE) . . . REMOVE THE GERM FROM GARLIC . . . COOK SPICES . . . BOIL OFF ALCOHOL . . . COOK TO PLEASE YOURSELF AS YOU MIGHT WRITE OR PAINT, DANCE OR SING TO PLEASE YOURSELF . . . CREATE YOUR OWN THEFTS . . .

tripe? His beam became a grin: the normal way, of course, just like every-one else. He shook my hand and returned to his kitchen. This man had the right idea.

This recipe is a combination of guesswork and theft, notably from la Confrérie des Tripaphages de Château Gontier, a town on the Mayenne north of Angers. Members of this chapter, presumably single-issue fan-atics, wear velvet gowns and carry scrolls of what appear to be leatherette parchment.

IKG COOKED TRIPE CUT INTO SMALL SQUARES

4 SHALLOTS

75CL FLEMISH BROWN BEER: CAROLUS, MAREDSOUS, CHIMAY,
    LA CHOUFFE, ETC.

DESSERTSPOONFUL BROWN SUGAR

IOCL SWEET VINEGAR

4 SLICES PAIN D'ÉPICES, CRUMBLED

PINCH OF POWDERED CLOVE

Cook the chopped shallots over low heat for 30 minutes or until soft. Add the rest of the ingredients. Bring to the boil for a minute or two to burn off the alcohol then turn down heat to a simmer. Cook for approximately 2 hours – it depends on the degree to which the tripe has been precooked. It is important to check.

TRIPE AND CELERY

This isn't trippa alla Romana. It omits tomato, hot peppers and carrots which get in the way of that dish's unusual combination of celery and mint.

IKG COOKED TRIPE CUT IN SMALL SQUARES

6 STICKS CELERY

6 CLOVES GARLIC

1 ONION

1 END OF RAW HAM

75CL DRY WHITE WINE

MINT

Cook the onions and garlic till soft then add the celery, chopped into pieces 4cm long, for a few minutes. Pour in the wine and bring to the boil for a couple of minutes. Add the tripe and the ham. Cook at a low temperature for 2 hours. It may need longer. Just as it is about to be served throw in several handfuls of chopped mint.

The more elaborate a country's table manners the worse its cooking.

TRIPE: APPROXIMATELY ASTURIAN

1KG COOKED TRIPE CUT INTO 4CM SQUARES

PIPERADE (P. 132)

200G RAW HAM

200G SMOKED AND DRIED ASTURIAN MORCILLA

200G PIQUANT CHORIZO

PIMENTON PICCANTE

50CL LIGHT STOCK

25CL DRY WHITE WINE

Bring the stock and wine to the boil. Turn down to a simmer. Add the tripe mixed with the piperade (made with pimenton piccante rather than piment d'Espelette), the ham, the chorizo and the Asturian morcilla: this is intensely flavoured and suitable only for dishes of this sort. Raw or

'SEASON ... SALT ... MAYBE PEPPER (CAN BE WHITE) ... REMOVE THE GERM FROM GARLIC ... COOK SPICES ... BOIL OFF ALCOHOL ... COOK TO PLEASE YOURSELF AS YOU MIGHT WRITE OR PAINT, DANCE OR SING TO PLEASE YOURSELF ... CREATE YOUR OWN THEFTS ...

fried it is a bit of a buccal challenge. It should be cut into slices of about 2cm.

Cook for a couple of hours.

SHAD ROE / LAITANCE D'ALOSE

If you can get it . . . Shad are found in the Severn and its affluents the Wye and the Teme. Also in the Gironde which, like the Severn, is tidal and has a bore (*le mascaret*). The fish are migratory. The Bordelais practice is to grill them over sarments, i.e. vine twigs. Beware, a shad is as bony as a pike. The idea that the bones will be dissolved by stuffing it with sorrel is an old wives' tale. The primary gastronomic excitement of the shad is its roe, which is at its best just before spawning in early summer.

To make shad 'caviar' remove the roe from its sacs and mix with coarse salt. Put in a fridge for several hours, then rinse it very thoroughly. Add the juice of a lemon (which will remove the brownish red colour) and a little walnut oil. Serve as a 'sauce' for pasta or on toast.

The roe can equally be gently fried or grilled. Take care since the sac is likely to break if too much heat is applied.

HERRING ROE

FLOUR SEASONED WITH PEPPER, PIMENTON PICCANTE,
RAS EL HANOUT

SOFT ROES

Roll the roes in the flour. Fry in hot oil for a couple of minutes.

CHICKEN LIVER PÂTÉ

500G CHICKEN LIVERS

2 CLOVES GARLIC

1 ONION

50CL CREAM

20CL MONBAZILLAC

CHILLI INFUSED OIL

Fry the diced onion and garlic gently, then turn up the heat and add the trimmed chicken livers till they are coloured – about 3 minutes. Process them. Add first the cream, then the wine. Watch out: don't let it get too liquid.

Never use English sausage 'meat'. If an English sausage is slurry in a condom, English sausage 'meat' is unprotected slurry. Beware: Sausage Transmitted Diseases are epidemic. Mince some pork yourself. And remember, don't be fooled – a chipolata is slurry in a kiddy's condom.

CHICKEN LIVER SOUFFLÉ

In Lyon, of which it is a native, this dish goes under the name of gâteau de foies blonds, which perhaps sounds more appetising. Georges Blanc's Ancienne Auberge at Vonnas, 50km north of the city, is the over-restored Germolene-pink Fabrique de Limonade which was run by his grandparents. The recipes pretty much date from the earlier decades of the 20th century. The gâteau is a culinary marvel, unbeatable – which is precisely why I haven't nicked his recipe and propose one that includes eggs, which he omits.

'SEASON . . . SALT . . . MAYBE PEPPER (CAN BE WHITE) . . . REMOVE THE GERM FROM GARLIC . . . COOK SPICES . . . BOIL OFF ALCOHOL . . . COOK TO PLEASE YOURSELF AS YOU MIGHT WRITE OR PAINT, DANCE OR SING TO PLEASE YOURSELF . . . CREATE YOUR OWN THEFTS . . .

250G CHICKEN LIVERS

125G CRUSTLESS BREAD

50CL MILK

3 EGGS

30CL CREAM

I CLOVE GARLIC

I SHALLOT

BUTTER

Prepare a bain marie. Butter 6 ramekins of about 12cm diameter. Soak the bread in the milk. Wring out. Separate the eggs. Clean the livers, pulling out the nerves. Put the livers, the bread, the egg yolks, the cream, the garlic and the shallot into a processor. Homogenise. Remove to a bowl. Beat the egg whites till they are stiff. Fold into the mix dexterously. Fill the ramekins and put in the bain marie. The water should come about two-thirds of the way up their side.

Cook at 130°C for 30 minutes. Unmould the soufflés. Serve with Tomato sauce 2 (p. 27).

SANGUETTE

It's up to the curious reader to track down a supply of fresh blood – chicken, duck, guinea fowl or pig. Offering your body to abattoir workers will usually do the trick. Raising the birds and animal yourself is a possibility. Dried pig's blood is available from: **www.weschenfelder.co.uk** (this Teesside company also sells sausage casings, brine, cures, etc.).

Sanguette used to be widely available in France, specifically in what was Occitania, i.e. roughly the southernmost third of the country. Today, because stringent laws govern the slaughter of animals, it is only to be found under the counter in country markets.

There is a misapprehension that it is some sort of omelette.

It is very easy to make.

BASICS ARE ON PP. 11–23 ... DON'T WALK AWAY ... CONCENTRATE ... FUCK THE GUESTS ... AND ALL THAT CONVIVALITY MALARKY ... DO NOT WASTE BREAD: OIL IT AND REBAKE IT ... STOCK! GET TREATMENT FOR SQUEAMISHNESS ... VEGETARIANISM IS CURABLE'

BLOOD

VINEGAR

BREADCRUMBS

GARLIC, CHOPPED

ONION, CHOPPED

PARSLEY, CHOPPED

DUCK FAT

Add a few drops of vinegar to the blood. This will prevent it curdling. Sweat the onion and garlic in duck fat at a low temperature till they are soft. Mix the blood with the breadcrumbs. Add a bit more fat, turn up the heat and put in the blood and breadcrumbs. Turn once. If turning it presents a problem cook it in a high oven. It is done when it has solidified. You can eat straightaway or leave it to cool and later reheat it.

EUPHEMISMS

Blandine Vié's *Testicules* is Englished as *Testicles: Balls in Cooking and Culture* (Prospect Books). Giles MacDonogh, who translated it, rather astonished me with the intelligence that this delicacy of many names – joyeuses, rognons blancs, valseuses, amourettes, coquilles, etc. – is available from two butchers within a few minutes of his home in north London: Harry in Kentish Town and Cramer in York Way. Now, north London is evidently atypical of England but I am prompted to wonder if balls are not quite as difficult to find as I believed them to be.

BALLS

OIL/BUTTER

BREADCRUMBS SEASONED WITH POWDERED CUMIN

Whether they belonged to a sheep, a calf or a bull, the preparation is the

'SEASON ... SALT ... MAYBE PEPPER (CAN BE WHITE) ... REMOVE THE GERM FROM GARLIC ... COOK SPICES ... BOIL OFF ALCOHOL ... COOK TO PLEASE YOURSELF AS YOU MIGHT WRITE OR PAINT, DANCE OR SING TO PLEASE YOURSELF ... CREATE YOUR OWN THEFTS ...

same. The outer membranes must be removed (if the butcher hasn't done so). Then blanch them.

Fry them in breadcrumbs.

The flavour is close to that of sweetbreads and like sweetbreads they are better without sauce.

SWEETBREADS

SWEETBREADS

SEASONED FLOUR

I EGG

Soak the breads in cold vinegared water. Remove as much membrane as possible. Blanch them for 15–20 minutes in barely simmering water. Remove remaining membrane. Allow them to cool. Cut them into slices 1cm thick. Put into beaten egg. Dredge in seasoned flour. Fry in a mix of butter and sunflower oil, 3 minutes each side. Serve without sauce.

Jules Gouffé, *officier de bouche* at le Jockey-Club de Paris, wrote in the preface of *Le Livre de Cuisine* (1867): *I have for many years hesitated (to write this book) because of the uselessness of the majority of such books which are nothing but servile copies of each other repeating the same vague and often incorrect . . .*

The prescient M Gouffé evidently had me in mind.

BRAINS WITH BROWN BUTTER

This is the only way to serve brains (and, for that matter, skate). In both instances brown butter is de rigueur and unimprovable.

Calves' brains are larger and less fiddly than lambs'.

BRAINS

BUTTER

VINEGAR

CAPERS

Put the brains in cold, salted, acidulated water for half an hour. You now need a dexterous, unsqueamish and preferably stoned kitchen intern to peel off the membrane and excise bone shards. This is time-consuming.

Put the brains in more cold, salted, acidulated water. Bring gently to a simmer. Poach them for 15 minutes.

Allow them to cool. Remove any bits of membrane that remain.

Cut into slices about 8mm thick.

Fry gently in butter till they are beginning to colour. Take off the heat. Add more butter to the pan and cook till it starts to turn brown. Throw in capers and sweetish vinegar – Chardonnay or Pedro Ximenez. Let this come to a bubble. Pour it over the brains.

LAMB HEARTS

LAMB HEARTS

SPICED OIL

Slice hearts as close to wafer-thin as possible. Heat spiced oil till it's smoking.

Put in the slices of heart. Cook for a minute. Turn them and cook for another minute.

Sprinkle lightly with vinegar.

'SEASON ... SALT ... MAYBE PEPPER (CAN BE WHITE) ... REMOVE THE GERM FROM GARLIC ... COOK SPICES ... BOIL OFF ALCOHOL ... COOK TO PLEASE YOURSELF AS YOU MIGHT WRITE OR PAINT, DANCE OR SING TO PLEASE YOURSELF ... CREATE YOUR OWN THEFTS ...

CHITTERLINGS

In most of France pigs' intestines are used to make andouillettes. In Bordeaux and its immediate surrounds they are called tricandilles, a near homophone of chitterling, and are fried or grilled. Culinary localism (and incuriosity) in provincial France is so entrenched that only 50km from the city they are unknown.

When I described them to a village butcher in the Charente he somewhat bemusedly agreed to try to get me some. He succeeded. What he obtained were intestines that had not been cleaned. They were full of pig shit. Still, a powerful Kärcher did the trick. And, as a food-poisoned, vomiting, incontinent, tissueless American hippy on a jolting bus in Morocco told a friend of mine: 'You gotta eat a heap of shit before you die.'

CHITTERLINGS

DUCK FAT

PERSILLADE (P. 34)

Fry the chitterlings in hot fat till crisp. Sprinkle on persillade. They are delicious.

Chitterlings are available online from a number of farm shops in the west of England and from butchers: Pritchett in Salisbury, Cooper in Darlaston, Crump & Son in Wootton Bassett, Dalton in Bordeaux's twin town Bristol.

GAYETTES

Industrially produced English faggots are every bit as nasty as English sausages. The same foul unidentified meat-style swill, the same long deceased herbs, the same sawdust breadcrumbs bulking out the filth, the same intimation of a big ralph.

There are exceptions. Rather, there is one exception: Gary Rhodes is the only English pro chef capable of coming up with anything as richly savoury as the gayettes I buy from a zealously unsmiling charcutier in the market close to where I live. They are not difficult to make.

500G BELLY PORK

500G LEAN PORK

1KG PIG'S LIVER

1 PIG'S HEART

CAUL FAT

4 CHARD LEAVES

2 ONIONS

4 CLOVES GARLIC

GRATED NUTMEG

PIMENTON PICCANTE

RAS EL HANOUT

DUCK FAT

Put caul fat in lukewarm acidulated water.

Sweat the very finely chopped onions and the spices for 10 minutes over a low heat in duck fat. (The point is to cook the spices.)

Mince all the other ingredients coarsely. Dry the caul fat. Cut it with a very sharp knife or scissors. Spoon the mix onto pieces of caul fat that are large enough to thoroughly wrap round them, perhaps even double wrap. Cook them in a roasting tray smeared with duck fat for 90 minutes at 140°C. If necessary turn up the heat for a few minutes to brown them when they are nearly done.

'SEASON . . . SALT . . . MAYBE PEPPER (CAN BE WHITE) . . . REMOVE THE GERM FROM GARLIC . . . COOK SPICES . . . BOIL OFF ALCOHOL . . . COOK TO PLEASE YOURSELF AS YOU MIGHT WRITE OR PAINT, DANCE OR SING TO PLEASE YOURSELF . . . CREATE YOUR OWN THEFTS . . .

I just got to go and fry off some Spam for the old folks. Tich
– of Dave Dee, Dozy, Beaky, Mick and Tich – whose
post-pop career has been running a care home.

VEG

GRATIN DAUPHINOIS

No cheese. Rowley Leigh used to include a piquant soft goat cheese at Kensington Place. It made for a truly delicious dish – but it wasn't gratin dauphinois. Paul Bocuse includes Gruyère. Were they both wrong? Happily blessed with a certain obstinacy they'll both deny it till the goats and cows come home.

No cheese, then. Just:

POTATOES

GARLIC

CREAM

BUTTER

The potatoes must be waxy, not liable to collapse. Slice them 2–3mm thick. Use a processor if you have one. Butter a gratin dish; pour in 50cl cream. Crush four cloves of garlic and mix into the cream. Add the sliced potatoes, making sure that they all get coated. Dot the top with butter. Cook in a low oven (140°C) for 90 minutes.

POMMES BOULANGÈRES

There's absolutely no point in doing this unless you have a good stock. That means not using a stock cube. No point equally if you have potatoes that are floury and will fall apart.

STOCK – CHICKEN/BEEF/DUCK/PHEASANT

FIRM POTATOES

ONIONS

GARLIC

Slice onions and garlic. Season with ras el hanout, cumin, pimenton dulce.
Cook slowly in olive oil for 30–40 minutes. Do not let them colour.
Oil a gratin dish.
Slice potatoes thinly.
Layer the potatoes with onion and garlic.
Just about cover with stock.
Cook in a low oven for 60–90 minutes till the stock is close to being absorbed. The quality of the dish depends on the quality of the stock.

Onions and garlic that have been sliced but not cooked before being incorporated will change the character of this dish without notably improving it. It is supposedly so named because it originated in homes without cooking facilities where it would be put together before being taken for communal cooking in a baker's oven. It seems probable, then, that in those golden days when everyone was in it together and there was no sanitation the onion and garlic would not have been previously prepared. Authenticity is seldom worth pursuing; excellence always is.

POMMES ANNA

There was a glut of *grandes horizontales* named Anna during the Second Empire. There are then several claimants to the honour of having the dish named after them. The favourite is Anna Deslions, la Lionne des Boulevards.

'SEASON . . . SALT . . . MAYBE PEPPER (CAN BE WHITE) . . . REMOVE THE GERM FROM GARLIC . . . COOK SPICES . . . BOIL OFF ALCOHOL . . . COOK TO PLEASE YOURSELF AS YOU MIGHT WRITE OR PAINT, DANCE OR SING TO PLEASE YOURSELF . . . CREATE YOUR OWN THEFTS . . .

She was one of the era's most loved and most notorious courtesans. She was among Zola's models for Nana. Her preferred haunt was le Café Anglais on the boulevard des Italiens, as much an exclusive maison de rendezvous as a restaurant – it had 20 private rooms. It is presumed that it was for her that the chef, Adolphe Dugleré, created it.

This version, which replaces butter with duck fat, is an approximation of that done by Stephen Markwick, Bristol's finest-ever chef.

WAXY POTATOES

DUCK FAT

GARLIC

Slice potatoes very thinly in a processor or on a mandoline. Brush a gratin dish with melted duck fat. Arrange a layer of potatoes to cover the bottom. Brush it lightly with fat. Sprinkle with garlic. Another layer of potatoes ... and so on. Cook at 150°C for 50 minutes. The top should be crisp. To demould it, hold a plate larger than the cooking vessel over it and turn it upside down swiftly. It should come out more easily than when done with butter.

Do this in remembrance of me.

The central rite of the Christian church, the eucharist, is cannibalistic: what is eaten is not a symbol, it *is* the body and blood. Preposterous nonsense. The half-witted rite is also unvarying, that is its paramount characteristic. The communicant submits. Every eucharist copies the last eucharist. There is no place for improvisation: the Artotyrites, who celebrated with bread and cheese, were apostates.

Further, the 'wine' from Crediton is always disgusting. The whole sorry business gives plagiarism a bad name.

RÖSTI / POMMES PAILLASSON / GALETTES DE POMME DE TERRE

There is no consensus. According to the most celebrated of all Swiss chefs, Fredy Giradet, rösti are made with boiled potato while pommes paillasson are made with raw potato. But in Zurich rösti are made with raw potato . . . and the finest I've eaten was at Kronenhalle in that city, after an exhibition of my favourite painter. The finest pommes paillasson were from Olivier Traiteur at the Marché des Grands Hommes in Bordeaux; almost certainly cooked from raw.

POTATO

OLIVE OIL/PEANUT OIL/DUCK FAT

Grate the potato finely. Put in cold water. Wring it dry with your hands or in a clean cloth to get rid of the starch. Form the grated potato into discs of about 100mm diameter and no more than 12mm deep – this is important: a greater depth won't allow the centre to cook without the exterior burning. Put them in the hot oil/fat. Push down to make them bind. Lower the temperature. Cook for about 6–7 minutes on each side till crisp.

As usual there are many recipes that call for additions: raw ham, cheese, shallots and so on. As usual resist these adulterants.

LATKES

Proceed as above. When the grated potato has been dried add beaten egg. Fry.

SAUTÉ POTATOES

WAXY POTATOES

BUTTER/OLIVE OIL/SUNFLOWER OIL/DUCK FAT

GARLIC

PARSLEY

Do peel the potatoes – unpeeled potatoes are an abomination.

Do not blanch let alone boil them.

Cut them into pieces the size of a malnourished walnut. Sauté – which may not be the right word – in hardly moving oil/fat for 50 minutes then gradually increase the temperature. Turn every few minutes. Cook them for about 90 mins. At the very last minute add either a persillade, i.e. chopped parsley and garlic, or minced garlic alone.

A chef needs a philosophy. Len Clent, executive slalom chef at the Hotel Rebate Oak International in Solihull, shares his philosophy with the readers of Leamington Tatler: *My philosophy – the Clent family philosophy for generations now – is that you got to get yourself a philosophy.*

BRATKARTOFFELN MIT SPECK

WAXY POTATOES

SMOKED BACON OR HAM

(SUNFLOWER OIL – OPTIONAL)

Essentially the same method as for sauté potatoes. Smoked pork from Germany and the German-speaking Alto Aldige tends to be more assertively flavoured than British produce. Cut the fat from the bacon or ham and let it melt slowly in the pan. (Top up with sunflower oil if insufficient fat has been yielded.) Put in the potatoes. Cook at low temperature for an hour. When the heat is gently turned up add diced lean bacon or ham. Cook for a further 30 minutes when both potatoes and bacon will be crisp.

This is sometimes called speckkartoffeln, though that more commonly tends to signify small potatoes wrapped in thinly sliced smoked pork and roasted.

POTATO PURÉE

IKG POTATOES

250G BUTTER

30CL CREAM

50CL MILK

This is really a suspension of potatoes in butter and cream. Like the rest of the world I took this from Joël Robuchon though I have never read his recipe or tasted his (or his underlings') version. So I guess I picked it up on *le téléphone arabe*.

Cut the potatoes into even-sized pieces, put in cold water and bring to a light boil. When they are done drain them and put back in the pan on low heat to dry them. Stir so they don't catch. Put them through a ricer or a mouli-legumes and return to the pan. The ricer is less risky; the rotational action of a mouli may cause them to become glutinous. On no account use a processor.

Add chopped-up butter, hot milk and cream gradually, whisking minimally. The resultant purée will be so delicious that the thought of flavouring it should be instantly quashed . . .

Having said that, I used often to eat at a Bolognese restaurant in Rome called Colline Emiliane that served a notable Parmesan-flavoured purée. Also Simon Hopkinson's purée with saffron (and olive oil instead of butter) is the spud's bollocks.

'SEASON . . . SALT . . . MAYBE PEPPER (CAN BE WHITE) . . . REMOVE THE GERM FROM GARLIC . . . COOK SPICES . . . BOIL OFF ALCOHOL . . . COOK TO PLEASE YOURSELF AS YOU MIGHT WRITE OR PAINT, DANCE OR SING TO PLEASE YOURSELF . . . CREATE YOUR OWN THEFTS . . .

STUFFED TOMATOES
AND COURGETTES

8 LARGE BEEF TOMATOES OR COURGETTES

ANCHOÏADE OR TAPENADE (P. 34 & P. 34)

BREADCRUMBS

OLIVE OIL

Halve the tomatoes and deseed them – keep the seed and jelly so that it can loiter unloved in the fridge for a few weeks before developing mould and getting chucked. Stuff with tapenade or anchoïade: fill up every aperture, as the actress said to the bishop. In both cases the 'sauce' should be mixed 50/50 with breadcrumbs. Put them in an oiled gratin dish and spray with more oil. Cook at 140°C for 50 minutes. They are best eaten lukewarm.

Courgettes are susceptible to the same treatment. Cut in half lengthwise then incise them lengthwise as deeply as possible without puncturing the skin. The stuffing may require extra oil to make it pliable enough to push into the incisions. Cook for slightly longer than tomatoes: 60–65 minutes.

Poulet Marengo is a form of theft. It is conventionally ascribed to Napoleon's chef Dunand who is said to have created it for the future emperor on 14 June 1800, the eve of the battle of Marengo in Piedmont, with ingredients he had scrounged in a nearby village – chicken, crayfish, tomatoes, eggs. He naturally cut the chicken with a sabre. In fact Dunand was not yet in Napoleon's employ. Beyond that, the combination of chicken and crayfish predates the battle by several centuries. It was particularly popular in the Dauphiné, where Dunand happens to be a common surname, and the Dombes, whose countless ponds were the crayfish's habitat before their stocks were largely destroyed by Californian crayfish under the command of Richard Nixon, who introduced them in the early 1970s as a cash crop. The appeal is obvious: steal a dish, fix its composition, add a great name (Napoleon not Nixon, though there is little to choose between them) and a folksy story – thus lifting it from the vernacular store to the heights of the classic repertoire.

COURGETTE BEIGNETS

1 LARGE COURGETTE

200G FLOUR

3 EGGS

40G PECORINO ROMANO

1 SHALLOT

2 CLOVES GARLIC

15CL OLIVE OIL

Grate the courgette and wring out much of the water. Add the grated cheese, diced garlic and shallot. Beat together the flour, eggs and olive oil. Add the courgette mix.

Heat sunflower oil in a pan. Fry the mix dessertspoonful by dessertspoonful, flattening so each beignet is 2cm deep max.

ELEPHANT GRATIN

'Copy anyone but never copy yourself.' Picasso did not of course heed his own advice. Self-plagiarism is probably the most common form of plagiarism. The perpetrator fails to notice – for this or that tic has become a habit, an unacknowledged signature. Equally likely he hopes the world won't notice it. After all, it's just about not straying from one's familiar territory . . . Maybe comfort zones should be razed to the ground. The dedi-

'SEASON . . . SALT . . . MAYBE PEPPER (CAN BE WHITE) . . . REMOVE THE GERM FROM GARLIC . . . COOK SPICES . . . BOIL OFF ALCOHOL . . . COOK TO PLEASE YOURSELF AS YOU MIGHT WRITE OR PAINT, DANCE OR SING TO PLEASE YOURSELF . . . CREATE YOUR OWN THEFTS . . .

cated plagiarist should have no familiar territory of his own. Cuckoos do not favour one species' nest and young over another's. A jay's chicks taste little different to a chough's. The plagiarist should steal indiscriminately.

The Elephant earned his nickname at school in the further East End because of his exceptional clumsiness. This might be a bit of a calumny on elephants who are actually nimble creatures.

I confidently recalled that the dish that now bears his name was nicked word for word from *Mastering the Art of French Cooking (MAFC)* . . . Save that it turns out not to have been: the nearest thing in that magisterial and essential book is a gratin of potatoes, onions, anchovies, eggs and cream – evidently a relation of the Swedish Jansson's Temptation (p. 67) which, properly, uses sprats rather than the anchovies I prefer. It's not that near. So where did Elephant Gratin come from? My mother used to make it but she's not around to ask. Still I'd swear on her grave that she ascribed it to *MAFC*. Happily, she has no grave; her ashes were thrown into the river Nadder at its confluence with the Hampshire Avon. My then girlfriend Christine Wood suggests that it was an amalgam of the *MAFC* recipe and Jane Grigson's recipe for pissaladière. But cream and tomato in a pissaladière? My fear is that Christine or I or both of us invented it. Which is hardly the behaviour of plagiarists.

POTATOES – A FIRM VARIETY THAT WON'T FALL APART,
  SLICED ABOUT 4MM THICK

TAPENADE (P. 34)

TOMATO SAUCE I (P. 26), OMIT SALT

ANCHOÏADE (P. 34), OMIT VINEGAR

Oil a gratin dish or roasting tin with decent olive oil. Put in a layer of potatoes. Smear with tapenade. Another layer of potatoes, followed by tomato sauce, a further layer of potatoes, then anchoïade, then more potatoes. Spray the top with more olive oil.

Cook in an oven at about 180°C for 60–80 minutes.

It is equally good, maybe even better, served cold. The Elephant, who was staying because he was between flats, concurred. One day I made an inordinate quantity of it for a party of ten people the following evening. In the morning I wandered into the kitchen to make coffee. The roasting tin was empty save for a few drops of oil, a smear of tomato and a tide mark of potato crust. The Elephant was unabashed. He had been very hungry. He considered it the far side of delicious. I failed to accept his compliments with good grace.

ENDIVES 1

The emblematic torpedo-shaped vegetable of both Belgiums and of French Flanders. (Do not confuse with Batavian endive or escarole.) Francophones call it chicon, nederlandophones call it witloof. Whatever name it's going under it is unmissable. It is also versatile. Raw, it adds a bracing bitterness to salads.

ENDIVES

BUTTER

POWDERED CARAWAY

Cut each endive in two along its length. Spice them, and cook slowly in butter in a vessel with a tight-fitting lid – 140°C for 60 minutes.

Eat them as they are or use them in this simple dish:

4 BRAISED ENDIVES

40CL CREAM

300G GRATED GRUYÈRE

200G DICED RAW HAM

BREADCRUMBS

Put the endives in a buttered gratin dish. Coat them with a mixture of the cheese, cream and raw ham. Breadcrumbs on the top. Bake for 15 minutes at 220°C.

'SEASON ... SALT ... MAYBE PEPPER (CAN BE WHITE) ... REMOVE THE GERM FROM GARLIC ... COOK SPICES ... BOIL OFF ALCOHOL ... COOK TO PLEASE YOURSELF AS YOU MIGHT WRITE OR PAINT, DANCE OR SING TO PLEASE YOURSELF ... CREATE YOUR OWN THEFTS ...

The strongest poets . . . achieve a style that captures and oddly retains priority over their precursors . . . one can believe for startled moments, that they are being imitated by their ancestors. Harold Bloom, borrowing, without admitting to it, from J. L. Borges' niftier formulation: *Every writer creates his own precursors.*

ENDIVES 2

Slice them so thinly that they are all but shredded. Cook in chilli-infused oil till they wilt.

CEP TART

'The forest floor at Emery Down was a carpet of penny buns.'

In her dementia my mother's short-term memory was shot. As is usual in such cases she had perfect if increasingly repetitive recall of weekends three-quarters of a century before, when my grandparents would drive her and her sister, my future aunt, from Southampton in their newly acquired car to the New Forest, there to gather or hope to gather penny buns, a fungus that predates even Signor Carluccio. Today they are of course better known as ceps or cèpes or porcini on the grounds that they taste better if provided with a foreign handle. Ambling through woods on the qui vive for whatever they are called is pleasurable even when you encounter 'professional' pickers, sharp-faced bucolic low-lifes staggering under the weight of their baskets and greed. Were it not for this cadre of thieving bastards fancy restaurants would not be able to charge the earth for minute portions of fungi they don't know how to cook.

BASICS ARE ON PP. 11–23 . . . DON'T WALK AWAY . . . CONCENTRATE . . . FUCK THE GUESTS . . . AND ALL THAT CONVIVALITY MALARKY . . . DO NOT WASTE BREAD: OIL IT AND REBAKE IT . . . STOCK! GET TREATMENT FOR SQUEAMISHNESS . . . VEGETARIANISM IS CURABLE'

There are two things you can do with ceps. Whichever you choose, the fruitbodies must be cleaned. Don't wash them but wipe with a clean cloth. Cut away any bits with earth attached to them – use a very sharp knife. Cut away any bits that are damaged by worms.

The first option is to slice them and sauté them in duck fat (or butter and olive oil) and to powder them with persillade just before they are done – take care the garlic doesn't burn.

The second is to make a tart. This recipe is far simpler than any that I have read. As is so often the case, recipe writers – whether chefs or journalists – seem to reckon that adding ingredients adds value. This is very seldom the case.

> 500G CEPS
>
> 1 SHEET PURE BUTTER PUFF PASTRY
>
> GARLIC BUTTER
>
> EGG YOLK

Slice the ceps very thinly. Cover the pastry in layers of ceps leaving a border of about 2–3 cm. Paint the border with egg yolk. Cook at 200°C for 15–20 minutes. A couple of minutes before it's done lob on chunks of cold garlic/parsley butter.

PUFFBALL

Calvatia gigantea is the species you need. They are indeed gigantic. Some exceed a strapping beer belly's dimensions. Specimens 20cm in diameter are commonplace. They grow in grass – damp meadows, parks, gardens. They are only worth eating when absolutely fresh. The flesh must be entirely white.

All that is required is that they be cut into slices about 2cm thick and fried in butter and oil till they colour.

'SEASON . . . SALT . . . MAYBE PEPPER (CAN BE WHITE) . . . REMOVE THE GERM FROM GARLIC . . . COOK SPICES . . . BOIL OFF ALCOHOL . . . COOK TO PLEASE YOURSELF AS YOU MIGHT WRITE OR PAINT, DANCE OR SING TO PLEASE YOURSELF . . . CREATE YOUR OWN THEFTS . . .

An original artist is incapable of copying. To be original he has, then, only to copy. Jean Cocteau

ONION GRATIN

2KG ONIONS

50CL CREAM

2 EGGS

Sweat the thinly sliced onions in olive oil and butter at a low heat for about an hour. They must be soft and uncoloured. They will be considerably reduced. Allow them to cool. Butter a gratin dish. Beat the eggs with the cream. Add the onions. Bake in a medium oven for 40 minutes.

This is evidently tarte à l'oignon or zewelwai without pastry, which I initially omitted due to my dislike of touching wheat flour, in the process discovering that the filling without the casing is an improvement. Equally I do not use flour to absorb the oil and butter that the onions have been cooked in: this is, anyway, an unnecessary step, but one that every recipe includes because it is included in every preceding recipe. The simple lesson here is don't believe recipes: steal, yes – but question the value of what you have stolen. There is no more pathetic fate than that of the burglar whose life-changing Goya turns out to be fake.

PISSALADIÈRE

Over half a century ago, Elizabeth David rued both the scarcity of this tart and the tendency to call it pizza provençale which was, actually, hardly surprising for Provence challenges the Campania for primacy in pizza. Marseille is possibly the greatest city of the pizza: there are more than a

BASICS ARE ON PP. 11–23 . . . DON'T WALK AWAY . . . CONCENTRATE . . . FUCK THE GUESTS . . . AND ALL THAT CONVIVALITY MALARKY . . . DO NOT WASTE BREAD: OIL IT AND REBAKE IT . . . STOCK! GET TREATMENT FOR SQUEAMISHNESS . . . VEGETARIANISM IS CURABLE'

hundred mobile pizza vans. The variety may not be that of Naples but the standard is unquestionably higher because, by Neapolitan standards, the pizza is *incorrect*. It is often closer to a tarte fine than to a 'real' pizza. Better always trumps real. This version is better.

2KG SWEET ONIONS

400G ANCHOVIES

I SHEET PURE BUTTER PUFF PASTRY

BLACK OLIVES

OLIVE OIL

Cook the thinly sliced onions and half the anchovies at very low heat for 2 hours till the onions are reduced and very soft and the anchovies have dissolved.

Spread this mix on the pastry leaving a 1cm border. Brush the border with olive oil.

Decorate the top with the rest of the anchovies and the pitted olives. Bake in a medium oven for 20–25 minutes.

FARÇOUS

These belong to the Aveyronnais vernacular. Save at home I have not eaten them anywhere other than at La Taverne in Rodez, a fine paleolithic restaurant that no longer exists. Philippe Regourd sold it to a tyro. Within months it went into liquidation. This is one of several of M Regourd's dishes that I have stolen and amended. The quantities are, as usual, approximate.

4 CHARD LEAVES

I ONION

3 CLOVES GARLIC

HANDFUL OF PARSLEY

150G FLOUR

25CL MILK

2 EGGS

'SEASON ... SALT ... MAYBE PEPPER (CAN BE WHITE) ... REMOVE THE GERM FROM GARLIC ... COOK SPICES ... BOIL OFF ALCOHOL ... COOK TO PLEASE YOURSELF AS YOU MIGHT WRITE OR PAINT, DANCE OR SING TO PLEASE YOURSELF ... CREATE YOUR OWN THEFTS ...

Beat the eggs. Add the milk. Incorporate the flour.

Chop all the other ingredients finely and mix with the batter.

Heat duck fat or olive oil in a pan. Form the farçous by pouring in dessertspoonsful of the mix. Do not fry more than a couple at a time. Turn once. They should be crisp and brownish.

I am like the thieving magpie. I gather from here and there everything that pleases me and store it in my nest. The problem is to stir around all of these heteroclite things until out of them comes a book. Michel Tournier

---

SWISS CHARD GRATIN

Blettes or bettes have not really caught on in the UK. Nor for that matter in Switzerland. The etymology is murky. How a southern European relation of the beet got saddled with that moniker is a mystery. The white stems, boiled, are versatile. Dress them while still hot with a walnut oil vinaigrette. Or make this gratin.

IKG CHARD STEMS

500CL CREAM

350G LAGUIOLE OR SALERS (OR CHEDDAR)

250G ROQUEFORT

Cut the stems lengthwise and then across into pieces about 3cm long. Butter a gratin dish and place them in it. Grate the cheeses, or chop them into small dice. Mix with the cream, leaving aside 100g Laguiole. Spoon over the chard making sure every piece is thoroughly coated. Bake in a medium oven for 30 minutes. Sprinkle the top with the remaining 100g Laguiole. Turn up the heat towards the end or put the dish under the grill to brown.

BASICS ARE ON PP. 11–23 . . . DON'T WALK AWAY . . . CONCENTRATE . . . FUCK THE GUESTS . . . AND ALL THAT CONVIVIALITY MALARKY . . . DO NOT WASTE BREAD: OIL IT AND REBAKE IT . . . STOCK! GET TREATMENT FOR SQUEAMISHNESS . . . VEGETARIANISM IS CURABLE'

PIPERADE

Piperade is a stew of peppers, tomatoes and onions. It does not include eggs.

4 PEPPERS

4 TOMATOES

4 ONIONS

2 CLOVES GARLIC

PIMENT D'ESPELETTE

OLIVE OIL

Peel and deseed the tomatoes and peppers. Fry a dessertspoonful of piment d'Espelette in hot oil for a few seconds. Add the sliced onions, minced garlic and lower the heat. When they are beginning to get soft add the chopped peppers and tomatoes. Add more oil if needed. Cook for at least an hour. No trace of raw peppers' rather unpleasant flavour should be detectable.

This is when eggs can be incorporated. Best beaten so they result in something between an omelette and scrambled eggs. Further things to add at this stage are raw ham and croutons.

BLATHERER

'Andy Blatherer' was not his name. That, however, is all that I've changed. His other properties are as I observed them.

He worked in the media – a word that, as Graham Greene observed over 40 years ago, signifies nothing other than bad journalism. Greene might have added 'and pointless meetings'. Andy loved meetings. He justified his existence by attending numberless mind-numbing boredom fests. He also loved blathering (the sound of his own voice was the sweetest music he had ever heard), duplicity, owning several mobiles to blather into, jobbery, sycophancy (to those above him in the hierarchical, we're-all-on-given-names-terms structure of the media), belittlement (of those below him), inventing expenses, something for nothing, uncontrolled greed, sloth. He had what is called a healthy appetite – which means nothing of the sort, it means the opposite. His capacity for lunch was boundless. He would leave a lunch meeting to waddle to a lunch meeting. He was always up for elevenses and high tea and, yes, a snack or two in between. He weighed 20 stone, was constantly short of breath, popped Prozac, smoked heavily and looked about a decade and a half older than he was.

One day in 2000, having failed to get me to a meeting – 'we love the script . . . we are just looking at reconfiguring the conceptual problems you have with the top . . . which we love, it's just that . . .' – he came to my apartment to blather. He arrived about midday and blathered and blathered. I made it clear that I had no conceptual problems, whatever they might be. Hunger struck on the hour of 1 o'clock.

'Where shall we have lunch?' he asked. In those days Bermondsey Street had yet to become a second Shoreditch. There were no artisanal burger wran- glers, no bio-dynamic yoghurt weavers, no free-range falafel beardies, just greasy spoons, Wonderloaves by the yard and a reeking pub. He suggested, then, that he call a taxi to deliver us to some restaurant across the river in the City. I was still writing about restaurants; my enthusiasm for them was waning by the week; the last place I wanted to go to was a restaurant.

'I'll knock something up.'

Andy looked dubious.

I poured him wine in a glass that takes a third of a bottle and gave him some Parmesan biscuits (p. 153).

'Where did you get these?' he asked.

'Colette made them,' I replied, head in the fridge, as though in a Werrity.

'Delicious . . . Have you got any more?'

In the fridge I found a piece of end of beef rump, roasted rare but slightly burnt. A roast fennel. A chunk of Beenleigh Blue (the greatest of British blue cheeses), some hard-boiled eggs, a bottle of capers, a bottle of cornichons, a Cos lettuce, some decaying tomato sauce, etc.

In a cupboard there were anchovies.

I chopped up some almost stale bread and fried it.

I gave Andy some more biscuits and poured him another glass.

I pared off the burnt bits of meat, sliced it thinly, cut the cheese into

BASICS ARE ON PP. 11–23 . . . DON'T WALK AWAY . . . CONCENTRATE . . . FUCK THE GUESTS . . . AND ALL THAT CONVIVALITY MALARKY . . . DO NOT WASTE BREAD: OIL IT AND REBAKE IT . . . STOCK! GET TREATMENT FOR SQUEAMISHNESS . . . VEGETARIANISM IS CURABLE'

dice, made a vinaigrette with walnut oil, anointed the chopped lettuce with it, put the eggs through a slicer, chopped garlic, anchovies, cornichons and a shallot, removed the skin of mould from the tomato sauce, thought the better of it and binned it. I chucked in the croutons, sprinkled some capers. And placed the bowl on the table.

Andy was bumbling about on one of his mobiles.

I told him lunch was ready. He sat down with a phone clamped to his face like a maxillary prosthesis. He signed off. I used big Chinese kitchen spoons to serve him. He ate greedily and evidently appreciatively for several minutes then, between chomping mouthfuls, spoke in absolute earnest: 'This is terrific . . . Could you let me have the recipe'.

Thus 'A Blatherer' became our word for a hastily improvised salad. A tuna blatherer, a cheese blatherer, a chicken blatherer and so on.

Andy Blatherer died after a long lunch.

———————————

Chefs aspire to art by creating fatuous novelties, by plagiarising the very idea of authorship, by failing to realise that their job is to carry the baton. Which is not an ignoble task.

———————————

PUMPKIN PURÉE

PUMPKIN

BUTTER

MACE

Boil pumpkin chunks of roughly the same size so that they cook evenly. Drain them. Dry them in the pot they cooked in, turning so that they don't burn. Get as much water out of them as possible. Mash. Add butter gradually, whisking. Season with mace.

'SEASON . . . SALT . . . MAYBE PEPPER (CAN BE WHITE) . . . REMOVE THE GERM FROM GARLIC . . . COOK SPICES . . . BOIL OFF ALCOHOL . . . COOK TO PLEASE YOURSELF AS YOU MIGHT WRITE OR PAINT, DANCE OR SING TO PLEASE YOURSELF . . . CREATE YOUR OWN THEFTS . . .

CHAMPIGNONS À LA GREQUE

These used to be unavoidable, they were on the menu of every provincial hotel in France.

CHAMPIGNONS DE PARIS/BUTTON MUSHROOMS

SUNFLOWER OIL

TOMATO SAUCE 2 (P. 27)

Slice the fungus thinly. Fry very gently so that they hardly colour. Steep in sauce while still hot.

BRAISED LETTUCE

I ROMAINE OR 3 LITTLE GEMS

100G BUTTER

STOCK

CARAWAY SEEDS

If using Romaine (or Cos) trim and cut it in two, lengthways. If using Little Gem don't bother, just trim the end. Blanch in boiling water for 8 minutes. Put between two plates to squeeze out as much liquid as possible. Put in a covered pan with butter, a small glass of stock, caraway seeds. Cook for an hour at low heat.

The cook can only imitate. Plagiarism in its many degrees is a form of unspoken adoration, respectful love, doting emulation. You want to be the man who wrote that sentence, painted that damask drape. Get over it!

You want to be the man who cooked that pie. That's more like it . . .

SALADE MECHOUIA

One of the emblematic dishes of the Jewish pieds noirs, first encountered in a gloomy first-floor restaurant overlooking the Canal St Martin many years before that part of Paris had been socially cleansed to make way for dance studios and very important conceptual art spaces.

IKG GREEN PEPPERS (THE MUDDY COLOUR IS MORE
  PLEASING THAN A MIX WITH RED WOULD BE.
  HENCE, TOO, THE SMALL PROPORTION OF TOMATOES)
250G TOMATOES, HALVED
CHILLI OIL
OLIVE OIL
8 UNPEELED GARLIC CLOVES
POWDERED CORIANDER AND CARAWAY
RAS EL HANOUT

Grill the peppers till the skins are black. Packing them in a plastic bag to remove the skins is not enough. The plastic bag must go into the freezer. Leave it there for 15 minutes. They will then yield easily. Grill the tomatoes and garlic. Peel them. Get rid of pips, skins, germs. Heat a mix of chilli-infused oil and regular olive oil and add ras el hanout, coriander, caraway.

'SEASON . . . SALT . . . MAYBE PEPPER (CAN BE WHITE) . . . REMOVE THE GERM FROM GARLIC . . . COOK SPICES . . . BOIL OFF ALCOHOL . . . COOK TO PLEASE YOURSELF AS YOU MIGHT WRITE OR PAINT, DANCE OR SING TO PLEASE YOURSELF . . . CREATE YOUR OWN THEFTS . . .

Turn down heat, simmer the peppers, tomatoes and garlic very gently for
1 hour or more.

FIG AND HAM TART

8 FIGS

4 SLICES RAW HAM

SHEET OF PURE BUTTER PUFF PASTRY

FRESH GOAT CHEESE

CHESTNUT HONEY

DUCK FAT

Heat oven. Mix honey – there is no substitute for the peculiar asperity of
chestnut – with cheese to make a supple paste. Spread this on the pastry
leaving a 3cm border. Cut the ham into 2cm squares and distribute evenly
on the honey/cheese.

Halve the figs and place them skin-side down on the tart. Give them
a sprinkling of piment d'Espelette. Brush them and the pastry border with
melted duck fat. Bake at 200°C for 20 minutes.

Leave to cool.

Taste.

Chuck in bin.

This wreck of a dish derived from commonplace observation and dodgy
reasoning. Since raw ham is frequently served with raw fig it is surely not
that much of a step to deprive them of their rawness and cook them. The
mix of very mild goat cheese and honey was disastrous, and surprising –
for yoghurt or caillé with honey is delicious, though it is not habitually
subjected to an oven. The ham was the other side of al dente, the figs borderline emetic. Altogether this botched essay in *sucré-salé* was about on a par
with the creations devised by Timothy Spall's Aubrey at the Regret Rien
in Mike Leigh's *Life Is Sweet*. That restaurant deserved to bomb, whatever
the composition of its menu. I mean, the name! There is no crasser confes-
sion than *I regret nothing*. Only the doltishly insentient, the immemoriously

recidivist, the sociopathic and the smug regret nothing. I no doubt belong, in this instance, to one of those unhappy categories by not regretting having invented this dish. I do not regret it because it was a warning. Never create when you can steal. Never enter a restaurant that advertises its 'cuisine d'auteur' or 'creative cooking'.

Aubrey's menu at the Regret Rien included: Black Pudding and Camembert Soup, Saveloy on a Bed of Lychees, Liver in Lager, Pork Cyst, Clams in Ham with Pan-Fried Cockell-based Sauce, King Prawn (just one) in Jam Sauce, Duck in Chocolate Sauce, Tongues in a Rhubarb Hollandaise, Tripe Soufflé, Quails on a Bed of Spinach and Treacle, and Grilled Trotter with Eggs Over Easy.

> The literary plagiarist is not necessarily a failed writer, just a clumsy one who leaves his dandruff on the purloined page, there to be forensically examined. The culinary plagiarist should be exultant.

'SEASON ... SALT ... MAYBE PEPPER (CAN BE WHITE) ... REMOVE THE GERM FROM GARLIC ... COOK SPICES ... BOIL OFF ALCOHOL ... COOK TO PLEASE YOURSELF AS YOU MIGHT WRITE OR PAINT, DANCE OR SING TO PLEASE YOURSELF ... CREATE YOUR OWN THEFTS ...

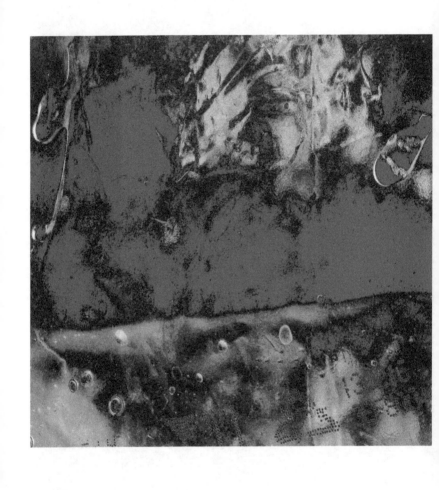

RICE, PASTA, ETC.

BASIC RISOTTO

Species snobbery is tiresome. The gastronomic approbation of the arcane, the artisanal, the local, the AOC, the sustainable, the scarce and the contempt for 'wasteful' air miles is frivolous: it's conventionalised fashion posing as ethical concern. Lives depend on the export of beans from Africa to a continent whose eaters preach seasonality but can't bear midwinter without strawberries and peaches.

Carnaroli, Vialone Nano and Baldo are, in that order, the most coveted varieties of risotto rice. So it is said. Arborio, the most frequently found and the cheapest variety, is apparently scorned by The Rice Community, no doubt because it *is* the most frequently found and the cheapest. It is supposedly liable to turn to mush faster than you can say Jack Robinson or *in men che non si dica.* I haven't found this to be the case.

What you do with the rice is more important than where it comes from.

What you do is keep patient.

What you do is stay put while it's cooking.

What you don't do is slip outside for a gasper with the other snoutcasts.

What you don't do is include wine. It adds nothing.

This is an elementary version, but then all risotti are easy so long as you concentrate.

300G ARBORIO RICE

3 ONIONS

3 CLOVES GARLIC

STOCK, SIMMERING

OLIVE OIL

BUTTER

In a mix of oil and butter sweat the finely chopped onions and garlic for 40 minutes. Use a heavy pan.

Add the rice. Turn it gently with a wooden spoon. When it is translucent turn up the heat just a little and pour in the first ladle of stock. When it has evaporated and been absorbed by the rice pour in the next. The risotto must never begin to get dry. Add too much rather than too little stock; rice is a sponge. But not so much of a sponge that it can be allowed to get malleable. Stir it now and then, judiciously: never use a fork. Do not get carried away stirring: cooking is not therapy. It should never attain more than a simmer. If it does the grains will cook unevenly, too soft on the outside, too hard within. The risotto will take about 30 minutes (many recipes state 20 minutes; they are wrong, they are cooking it at too high a temperature).

It's complete when the grains are al dente. Al dente does not mean that biting them will break your teeth, rather that there's a faint hint of resistance. The dish should be very slightly soupy; very slightly – balance is the thing.

CHICKEN AND MUSHROOM RISOTTO

ARBORIO RICE

(BONE MARROW, CHOPPED – OPTIONAL)

3 ONIONS, CHOPPED FINELY

3 CLOVES GARLIC, MINCED

BUTTER

OLIVE OIL

CARAWAY

'SEASON ... SALT ... MAYBE PEPPER (CAN BE WHITE) ... REMOVE THE GERM FROM GARLIC ... COOK SPICES ... BOIL OFF ALCOHOL ... COOK TO PLEASE YOURSELF AS YOU MIGHT WRITE OR PAINT, DANCE OR SING TO PLEASE YOURSELF ... CREATE YOUR OWN THEFTS ...

PIMENTON

STOCK, SIMMERING

2 CHICKEN BREASTS

BUTTON MUSHROOMS, SLICED

Chop the onions and garlic finely. Cook them for 40 minutes over low heat in a heavy pan in butter and oil to which caraway and pimenton have been added. (After 20 minutes put in the chopped bone marrow.)

Meanwhile poach the chicken breasts in the stock for 15 minutes. Chop them.

When the onions and garlic (and bone marrow) have melted, add the mushrooms and, as they are beginning to cook, add the rice, turning it gently till it becomes translucent.

Turn up the heat. Pour in a ladleful of stock. As soon as it has been absorbed pour in another. And another . . . Put in the chopped chicken breasts when there are about 10 minutes to go.

'Homemade' begs one question. Whose home? Have you ever actually seen people's homes? Why should biscuits made at home be better than those baked in a factory, a factory that specialises in biscuits? I'm thinking of Nairn's Oatcakes, Rakusen's Matzo Crackers and Carr's Water Biscuits. We don't seek treatment from amateur surgeons and Sunday dentists.

MILANESE RISOTTO

ARBORIO RICE

BONE MARROW, CHOPPED

3 ONIONS, CHOPPED FINELY

BUTTER

OLIVE OIL

SAFFRON

STOCK, SIMMERING

Sweat the onions in oil and butter for 40 minutes with the chopped bone marrow, which is all but obligatory.

Add the rice and cook till translucent. Begin to add stock by the ladle. Stir gently – easy, you know, does it, son. About 20 minutes after the rice has been added put the saffron into a heat-proof jug of some sort and fill the jug with stock. Pour this into the risotto. Don't let it get above a simmer. The scent is astounding. The colour dazzling. Do not add grated cheese. It fights the flavour of the saffron. Garlic is omitted for the same reason.

BLACK RISOTTO

This usually accompanies grilled squid or steamed octopus. It is perhaps better by itself.

300G ARBORIO RICE

3 ONIONS

6 CLOVES GARLIC

2/3 SACHETS SQUID INK

STOCK

CHILLI-INFUSED OIL

PECORINO ROMANO

Sweat the finely diced onions and garlic in chilli oil.

Add the rice in the usual fashion. Ditto the stock. When it is close to being cooked, put the ink into a pan and dilute with simmering stock. Pour this into the risotto. Continue to cook. Add grated Pecorino just before it's finished.

'SEASON...SALT...MAYBE PEPPER (CAN BE WHITE)...REMOVE THE GERM FROM GARLIC ...COOK SPICES...BOIL OFF ALCOHOL...COOK TO PLEASE YOURSELF AS YOU MIGHT WRITE OR PAINT, DANCE OR SING TO PLEASE YOURSELF...CREATE YOUR OWN THEFTS...

How boring it is to write recipes when one's job is to make them less than boring.

RISOTTO CAKE WITH CHEESE

300G ARBORIO RICE

3 ONIONS

3 CLOVES GARLIC

STOCK

PARMESAN, GRATED

PECORINO ROMANO, GRATED

GORGONZOLA, CUBED

CREAM

When the rice has been cooking for about 15 minutes add the Gorgonzola and Parmesan cheeses. It may be necessary to increase the amount of stock.

Five minutes from the end of cooking, stir in cream.

Put it into a buttered gratin dish. Sprinkle the top with Pecorino. Cook in a hot oven for 15 minutes.

ARANCINE / SUPPLI

The first name is Sicilian, the latter Roman. They are fine shallow-fried – as the son of a chip-pan incendiarist that is the only form of frying I dare undertake. If you have the nerve and a watertight insurance policy by all means try deep-frying them at home. Or you could buy a Philips Airfryer or Tefal Actifry to achieve the Vatican-approved deep-frying equivalent of safe sex.

Decent quality mozzarella is good as it is. No mozzarella gains from being cooked and turned to rubber. These croquettes are, then, not the *real* thing. They are better. (I am reminded of John Diamond's all too true observation that 'You don't want to live anywhere near *real* people'.)

They are oblongs rather than balls because that shape makes them easier to shallow fry.

500G BASIC RISOTTO

400G VEAL, FINELY CHOPPED OR COARSELY MINCED

BUTTER

15CL STOCK

15CL WHITE WINE

125G ROQUEFORT, CHOPPED

125G SALERS OR LAGUIOLE, CHOPPED

100G PECORINO ROMANO, GRATED

3 EGGS

FINE BREADCRUMBS

Gently cook the veal in butter, wine and stock till all the liquid has evaporated and the meat is just getting coloured – about 25 minutes. Let it cool. Mix in the Roquefort and Salers.

Beat 2 eggs and combine with the risotto and the grated Pecorino.

Form the risotto mix into oblongs 5cm long × 5cm wide × 4cm deep. Cut each one in half lengthways so there are two halves of 2cm depth. Hollow out some of the rice from each half. Fill the consequent hole with the veal/Roquefort/Salers. Press the two halves together. Repeat till you have used all the rice. With the rice that has been hollowed out fashion another couple of croquettes.

Brush each croquette with the third egg, beaten. Roll them in fine breadcrumbs.

Fry in hot oil, turning till every surface is well coloured.

'SEASON . . . SALT . . . MAYBE PEPPER (CAN BE WHITE) . . . REMOVE THE GERM FROM GARLIC . . . COOK SPICES . . . BOIL OFF ALCOHOL . . . COOK TO PLEASE YOURSELF AS YOU MIGHT WRITE OR PAINT, DANCE OR SING TO PLEASE YOURSELF . . . CREATE YOUR OWN THEFTS . . .

TV chefs are the enemies of proper cooking. Cooking is not an entertainment. There were two exceptions. Keith Floyd was unquestionably the best of the lot, not because he was a good chef – he wasn't – but because he was a small-town lothario whose charm the camera loved, a peculiar showman. Jennifer Paterson was also a tremendous turn. The rest are crass tossers with the spray-on grins, gestures and catch-phrases of the wretchedly, desperately, aspirantly characterful. Their forced enthusiasm fails to dissemble their catastrophic lack of humour. Like most television performers they prompt nothing but embarrassment. One cannot but wonder: do I really belong to the same species of animal as these joyless poots?

SPAGHETTI AND POUTARGUE CREAM

I ONION

4 CLOVES GARLIC

30CL CREAM

400G SPAGHETTI

5CL CHILLI-INFUSED OLIVE OIL

30G POWDERED POUTARGUE

Sweat onion and garlic in a pot big enough to hold the cooked spaghetti. When soft, add the cream and chilli oil. Bring just to boil. Add the poutargue. When the spaghetti is cooked drain it, keeping back a little of its liquid. Add the spaghetti to the cream and poutargue, stir tenderly. Use a drop or two of the spaghetti water to dilute the sauce if needed.

MIGAS

In *Tristana* Luis Buñuel shot the most sumptuous gastronomic sequence in all cinema. The young Tristana and the bell ringer eat migas which the latter has prepared. The frying pan is on the simple table. They eat with spoons. Food has never looked so delicious, so elemental on screen. Catherine Deneuve noted later that it was difficult to play the scene while eating.

Migas are 'crumbs', sometimes literally so, sometimes, as in this instance, croutons made with stale bread. They are, or were, the food of the poor – a staple (if lucky) to which might be added whatever was available (not much): the same goes for pasta, rice, potatoes, dumplings, etc. Migas are particularly associable with Extremadura in Spain's wild west. It was here, in the northernmost part of Caceres province that, almost 40 years before *Tristana*, Buñuel shot *Las Hurdes*, aka *Land Without Bread*, his documentary depiction of rural poverty's assault on the human spirit. Today Caceres does have bread. It is a roaring cowtown, a riotously affluent place. When my daughter Lily and I arrived there early one evening there were hundreds of people drinking beer in the main square. What's going on, I asked, is it a feast day? The barman was puzzled by my question. No, no it's not a feast day, why do you ask?

Well, the bacchanal . . .

Ah. No – it's always like this.

Migas are rather less humble than they once were. Indeed, they are to be found on the menus of the Michelin-approved restaurants that, Buñuel claimed, determined his locations: he liked to eat well after a hard day's blasphemy.

This suggestion approximates to somewhere between the utter simplicity of the dish in *Tristana* and a jazzed-up version I ate in one of Caceres's less chichi restaurants.

> 250G STALE BREAD WITHOUT CRUST
>
> 25CL MILK
>
> 30G PORK SAUSAGE – PROPER, NOT ENGLISH, NEVER ENGLISH
>
> 30G MORCILLA
>
> 30G HAM
>
> HAM FAT

'SEASON . . . SALT . . . MAYBE PEPPER (CAN BE WHITE) . . . REMOVE THE GERM FROM GARLIC . . . COOK SPICES . . . BOIL OFF ALCOHOL . . . COOK TO PLEASE YOURSELF AS YOU MIGHT WRITE OR PAINT, DANCE OR SING TO PLEASE YOURSELF . . . CREATE YOUR OWN THEFTS . . .

Soak the bread overnight in the milk. Wring it out. Fry the ham fat to release fat to fry in. Fry diced ham, crumbled sausage, little chunks of morcilla. Add oil to the pan if needed. Fry the bread.

Before the actors arrived Buñuel would go to the set with his lighting cameraman. They would discuss where tracks might be laid. They would plan where a jib might be used. They would think about a crane . . . and then they'd both fall about laughing, put down the camera on its legs and let the actors get on with it.

In the same spirit, just fry some bits of bread and eat them.

Everything in moderation – apart from excess. (I've reached an age when, regrettably, I no longer believe that.)

CADE / CALENTICA / FARINATA / PANISSE / SOCCA

These savoury 'breads' are all made with chickpea flour. Cade is Toulonnais. Calentica is the pied noir name: it was the street snack of Oran. Farinata is Genovese. Panisse is Marseillais. Socca belongs to Nice.

The proportions are the same for all of them.

Cade, calentica, farinata and socca are prepared thus:

400G CHICKPEA FLOUR

80CL WATER

10CL OLIVE OIL

(CUMIN SEEDS)

Make a batter adding the water bit by bit to the flour then mixing in half the oil. Let this stand for several hours or overnight.

Oil as big a pan as you have, or several pans. Heat them. The oven must be very hot. Pour in the batter. The depth should be no more than 2.5cm. Scatter over the cumin seeds if you fancy it. Rosemary, which I would never include, is sometimes used. Cook for 10–15 minutes till golden and crisp. The inside however should be yielding. Eat warm.

Panisse batter does not rest overnight. It is cooked in the pan in which it has been mixed. Stir it constantly. Allow it to heat till it comes away from the sides of the pan. Pour it onto a large sheet of greaseproof paper and roll it to form a cylinder. Or line an oblong terrine dish with the paper and shape the panisse accordingly. Let it get cold. Slice it into discs about 7mm thick. Fry in olive oil.

'SEASON . . . SALT . . . MAYBE PEPPER (CAN BE WHITE) . . . REMOVE THE GERM FROM GARLIC . . . COOK SPICES . . . BOIL OFF ALCOHOL . . . COOK TO PLEASE YOURSELF AS YOU MIGHT WRITE OR PAINT, DANCE OR SING TO PLEASE YOURSELF . . . CREATE YOUR OWN THEFTS . . .

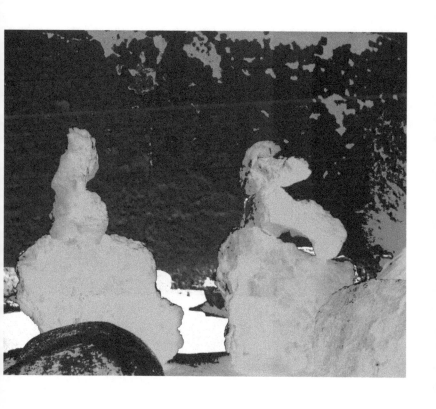

CHEESE

CHEESE TUILES

100G SALERS OR LAGUIOLE OR COMTÉ

100G PECORINO ROMANO OR PARMESAN

Grate the cheeses. Lightly oil a baking tray. Form the cheese, which should be adhesive, into wafer-like discs 8cm diameter, 2mm deep. Blitz in a hot oven for 4 minutes.

As someone who enjoys eating alone with a book I am suspicious of the notion that conviviality, friendship, hail-fellow-well-met good cheer, sharing, back-slapping bacchanals are necessarily the invariable concomitants of sitting at a table.

PARMESAN BISCUITS

A variation on Simon Hopkinson's recipe.

100G COLD UNSALTED BUTTER

100G PLAIN FLOUR

PIMENT D'ESPELETTE

SMALL SPOONFUL OF POWDERED MUSTARD

50G GRATED SALERS

50G GRATED PARMESAN OR PECORINO ROMANO

Mix all the ingredients in a processor. Use the pulse in short spurts to combine them. They will form a dough without the need for liquid. Wrap in clingfilm and roll into a cylinder of 25mm diameter. Chill for an hour or so. Cut the cylinder into slices 8mm thick. Place the biscuits on an oiled baking tray, 2cm apart, and cook at 180°C for 10 mins.

REBARBE

There are numerous sorts of rebarbe; by-products of cheese-making or mixtures of stale cheeses moistened with wine or distillates.

Philippe Regourd's 'recipe' for this fromage fort at La Taverne changed constantly – yet it was always pretty much always the same, constantly delicious.

750G ROQUEFORT

150G BUTTER

150G CREAM

50CL EAU DE VIE (VIEILLE PRUNE, MIRABELLE, QUETSCH,
    KUMMEL, ETC.) OR FORTIFIED WINE (PORT, PEDRO
    XIMENEZ) OR SWEET WINE (CADILLAC, ST CROIX DU
    MONT) OR PASTIS – OR A MIXTURE OF THESE.

Put the ingredients through a processor. Leave in the fridge for at least a week. Spread on good bread.

'SEASON ... SALT ... MAYBE PEPPER (CAN BE WHITE) ... REMOVE THE GERM FROM GARLIC ... COOK SPICES ... BOIL OFF ALCOHOL ... COOK TO PLEASE YOURSELF AS YOU MIGHT WRITE OR PAINT, DANCE OR SING TO PLEASE YOURSELF ... CREATE YOUR OWN THEFTS ...

Fast food is fat food with a sibilance problem. Fast food, 'convenience' food, is at one pole of invention. At the other is self-congratulatory, boastfully responsible sustainability – eco this, bio that, green and organic and friendly to the earth which, being inanimate, has no idea that dunces are cosying up to it. Nothing is sustainable. To claim otherwise is to deny entropy, to ignore dust's inevitability and to hope for everlasting life – you won't get it.

ROQUEFORT BISCUITS

50G ROQUEFORT

50G FLOUR

2 EGG WHITES

30G BUTTER

3CL OLIVE OIL

PIMENT D'ESPELETTE

Mix the ingredients till a smooth paste is formed. Put tablespoonsful on lightly oiled aluminium on a baking tray. Since the mixture will spread as it cooks allow a generous distance between each biscuit-to-be. Bake at 200°C for 12 minutes. Leave for at least 4 hours before eating them.

VACHERIN

500G RATTE POTATOES

CARAWAY SEEDS

VACHERIN

BASICS ARE ON PP. 11–23 ... DON'T WALK AWAY ... CONCENTRATE ... FUCK THE GUESTS ... AND ALL THAT CONVIVIALITY MALARKY ... DO NOT WASTE BREAD: OIL IT AND REBAKE IT ... STOCK! GET TREATMENT FOR SQUEAMISHNESS ... VEGETARIANISM IS CURABLE'

EAU DE VIE/WHITE WINE/SAKE

OLIVE OIL

Leave the cheese in its box. Make some incisions on top. Pour in white wine or eau de vie or even sake. Cook for 35 minutes at 200°C. Exceptionally, do not peel the potatoes. Toss in olive oil and bake them in their skins. Slice them in half longways. Dip them in the fondant cheese. Sprinkle with the caraway seeds.

Cabri Ariegois is a goat milk's analogue of Vacherin, rather less rich, rather more expensive.

Rouault, Emma's father, sent Charles Bovary a yearly turkey in thanks for fixing his broken leg. This is not a sign of the farmer's lack of imagination, rather of habit – which is more potent than imagination in the straitened circumstances of the bocage where the stimuli of imagination are few.

FRICO

This is a dish that appears not to have travelled far beyond Friuli and even there it's hardly commonplace. There are numerous ways of making it. Indeed the name is also attached to a dish of scalloped potatoes that bears no resemblance to the excellent version served at the Hotel Franz in Gradisca d'Isonzo, 40km north of Trieste. The balance of cheese and potato is crucial. The ordained cheese is Montasio – localism and all that. It is improbable that you'll find it in the UK. Saint Nectaire is the most reliable stand-in I've found but I guess Taleggio and Fontina would be OK.

'SEASON . . . SALT . . . MAYBE PEPPER (CAN BE WHITE) . . . REMOVE THE GERM FROM GARLIC . . . COOK SPICES . . . BOIL OFF ALCOHOL . . . COOK TO PLEASE YOURSELF AS YOU MIGHT WRITE OR PAINT, DANCE OR SING TO PLEASE YOURSELF . . . CREATE YOUR OWN THEFTS . . .

500G SEMI-HARD CHEESE, COARSELY GRATED

500G POTATOES, COARSELY GRATED

2 OR 3 BANANA SHALLOTS, FINELY CHOPPED

Cook the shallots till soft in plenty of butter. Add the potatoes and when they are getting soft add the cheese. Cook for about 20 minutes over a low heat or in a bain marie. The ingredients will eventually form a homogenous emulsion.

This can be fried in butter and olive oil – pour into a pan in which the mixture is about 3cm thick. Cook for 10 minutes then turn into another pan to brown the other side. That will probably mean dropping it on the floor. Hence screams and flying knives that reveal the plagiarist's streak of culinary psychopathy. (Clive Merrison once called me a kitchen fascist.) Safer perhaps to separate the mixture into small discs that are not a problem to turn over.

CAKE AUX OLIVES ET GRUYÈRE

250G PLAIN FLOUR

150G GRUYÈRE, GRATED

100G GREEN OLIVES, PITTED AND HALVED

4 EGGS

10CL OLIVE OIL

1 SACHET INSTANT YEAST

Heat oven to 180°C. Sift the flour and yeast into a bowl. Stir in the eggs and the olive oil. Add the olives, cheese and pepper. Mix well. Butter a loaf tin thoroughly, then add the mix. Cook for 45 mins. Cool before serving.

Vegetarians don't cook meat for you – so you must cook vegetables for them.

KHATCHAPURI

This cheese bread is inescapable in Moscow where every other restaurant is Caucasian. The most commonly used cheeses are Imeretian and Sulguni, which you are unlikely to find in the UK though the Russian shop at the Bayswater Road end of Queensway sometimes stocks the latter. Use ricotta, feta and mozzarella instead.

The dough:

200G SHEEP YOGHURT

2 EGGS

1 EGG YOLK

400G FLOUR

1 TSP BAKING POWDER

150G BUTTER

The filling:

200G RICOTTA

200G FETA

200G MOZZARELLA

Knead the dough ingredients apart from the egg yolk till they are homogenised. Refrigerate the dough.

Grate or chop the cheeses and mix them.

Roll out the dough to make two circles. Spread the cheese in the centre of one of them. Cover it with the second circle. Brush the top with egg yolk. Bake for 25 minutes at 220°C.

This 'pie' dough is also good filled with already-cooked lamb, minced and mixed with sweated onion.

'SEASON ... SALT ... MAYBE PEPPER (CAN BE WHITE) ... REMOVE THE GERM FROM GARLIC ... COOK SPICES ... BOIL OFF ALCOHOL ... COOK TO PLEASE YOURSELF AS YOU MIGHT WRITE OR PAINT, DANCE OR SING TO PLEASE YOURSELF ... CREATE YOUR OWN THEFTS ...

MUNSTER AND CUMIN

In the late Nineties we were eating lunch in Bofinger. Alone at the next table there was one of the many thousands of good-looking, vain Frenchmen who can't understand why they are not Alain Delon – it has something to do, no doubt, with their not possessing that actor's glacial poise and menacing blankness. This party noticed that I was eyeing the cheese he was served. It was accompanied by a petri dish of cumin or caraway seeds.

Would I like to try it? he asked.

I acknowledged his generosity.

He told me it reminded him of home: Strasbourg.

Do you often get back there? I asked.

He looked puzzled. I live there, he said.

It seemed odd that he should eat one of the vernacular confections of his home when in Paris – but I had not then any conception of the depth of unselfconscious French regional tribalism.

Not as odd as this though: he smiled slyly. Are you interested in painting?

Depends what painting . . .

What would you like to own?

Was this some sort of parlour game, I wondered.

If you could have anything . . .

Oh, let's say something by Dix or Scholtz, Beckmann.

Beckmann? I can get a Beckmann for you. No problem.

Really?

Really. More cheese?

Art thief? Fence? Fantasist? Fantasist.

He handed me his card: he grinned, get in touch.

I didn't. But I never eat Munster and caraway without thinking that I might just have become the owner of a stolen Grosz or a fake Oelze or the patsy in some sort of smiler's scam.

Ask not what you can do for your country. Ask what's for lunch. Orson Welles

---

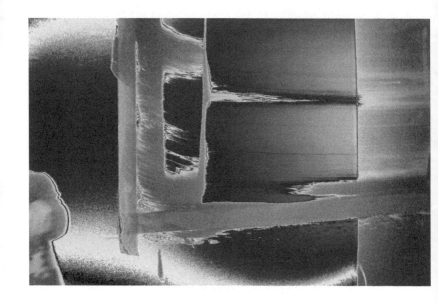

DESSERT

DRIED AND GLACÉ FRUIT SALAD

EAU DE VIE

SWEET WINE

Dried fruit:

FIGS

DATES

PRUNES

PINEAPPLE

Glacé fruit:

CLEMENTINES

MELON

ORANGE PEEL

GREENGAGE

ANGELICA

Chop all the fruits into small pieces. Put in a non-reactive bowl. Pour over the fruit a bottle of sweet wine (Loupiac, Cadillac, Monbazillac) and half a bottle of eau de vie (kirsch, mirabelle, poire). The fruit should be covered by the liquid. Leave to steep for 2 weeks.

PAIN PERDU

STALE BREAD

EGGS

MILK

VANILLA SUGAR OR SUGAR AND RUM

Make vanilla sugar by burying several vanilla pods in white sugar and leaving them in an airtight jar for a month.

If you can't be bothered mix sugar with rum or Spanish brandy – George Best's favourite drink among many favourite drinks: 'Yus, shewer, Oi loike ta slup dowun to the pooel fur a Fondador.'

The stale bread should be this side of Penicillium. Cut it into slices 2cm thick. Beat eggs, milk and sugar thoroughly. Steep the bread in it.

Fry the bread in butter that's close to burning. Sprinkle with more sugar.

Let my country die for me. James Joyce, *Ulysses.*

'SEASON ... SALT ... MAYBE PEPPER (CAN BE WHITE) ... REMOVE THE GERM FROM GARLIC ... COOK SPICES ... BOIL OFF ALCOHOL ... COOK TO PLEASE YOURSELF AS YOU MIGHT WRITE OR PAINT, DANCE OR SING TO PLEASE YOURSELF ... CREATE YOUR OWN THEFTS ...

BOREHAMWOOD ORANGES

Long Sunday lunches in the early Seventies meant the Pontevecchio in Old Brompton Road. Christine Wood and I, Tony Rivers and Ines Troeller, Jenny Harrington, Stephen Sheppard and that month's rich girl, Nigel Preston and Noni Buchan, Jenny Topper, John S—— aka MTF (Must Touch Flesh) who was twice our age, Duncan Browne, and another markedly less talented musician whom I once unintentionally insulted thus:

'I just can't think of a name for this new band we're getting together', he worried.

This was the era of Kilburn and The High Roads (prop: Ian Dury) and Hatfield and The North.

'What,' I suggested, 'about Borehamwood – We Bores You Stiff.'

He turned white with rage. Artists. So sensitive. He became a one-hit wonder – but what a hit, he made a fortune.

On another occasion an American academic at the next table told us that he had just returned from Mexico City, alive. What had most impressed him was the name of a brand of rat poison – The Last Supper.

Dessert was always:

8 ORANGES

GRATED ORANGE PEEL

ORANGEFLOWER WATER

ORANGE JUICE

500G SUGAR

50CL WATER

TRIPLE SEC/COINTREAU

Grate the oranges' peel, strip off pith, slice the oranges thinly against the grain, lay in a single layer in an oven dish.

Make a syrup with the water and sugar. When the sugar is dissolved and it begins to colour, pour the boiling syrup over the oranges.

When they are cold dress them with grated peel, orangeflower water, orange juice and Triple Sec or Cointreau.

PINEAPPLE BRAISED IN BEER

Provenance: I once overheard someone in a restaurant talking about having had this in another restaurant.

1 PINEAPPLE

BUTTER

TRIPEL BEER: WESTMALLE, MAREDSOUS, ST MARTIN, AFFLIGEM, ETC.

CORIANDER POWDER

CINNAMON

PIMENTON PICCANTE

Dice the pineapple. Gently fry the spices – no more than a pinch of each – in a little butter. Add the pineapple. Cook for about 10 minutes. Turn up the heat and pour in about 15–20cl of beer. Boil it. Turn down the heat, cover the pan, let it cook for 30 minutes. Take off the lid, allow the juices to caramelise. Best served warm.

'SEASON ... SALT ... MAYBE PEPPER (CAN BE WHITE) ... REMOVE THE GERM FROM GARLIC ... COOK SPICES ... BOIL OFF ALCOHOL ... COOK TO PLEASE YOURSELF AS YOU MIGHT WRITE OR PAINT, DANCE OR SING TO PLEASE YOURSELF ... CREATE YOUR OWN THEFTS ...

I got the idea of Loving *from a manservant in the Fire Service during the war. He was serving with me in the ranks, and he told me he had once asked the elderly butler who was over him what the old boy most liked in the world. The reply was: 'Lying in bed on a summer morning, with the window open, listening to the church bells, eating buttered toast with cunty fingers.' I saw the book in a flash.* Henry Green, *The Paris Review*, Summer 1958, No. 19.

BASICS ARE ON PP. 11–23 ... DON'T WALK AWAY ... CONCENTRATE ... FUCK THE GUESTS ... AND ALL THAT CONVIVALITY MALARKY ... DO NOT WASTE BREAD: OIL IT AND REBAKE IT ... STOCK! GET TREATMENT FOR SQUEAMISHNESS ... VEGETARIANISM IS CURABLE'

DRINK

SLOE VODKA

Sloes are available in some supermarkets and online. Still, there's a certain undemanding pleasure to be had in picking your own. It is pointless using gin, the flavour of whose botanicals will fight that of the sloes. Supermarket own-brand vodka is just the ticket.

VODKA OR ALCOOL POUR FRUITS

SLOES

SUGAR

Prick the sloes with a pin: another undemanding pleasure, which allows you to muse on ontological embuggerances. Fill about 40 per cent of a bottle with them. The amount of sugar you use depends on what style of drink you are after. You will certainly need some sugar because the fruit is fiercely tannic. But you don't want Malibu – do you? In any case you need to leave the liquor for 6 weeks at least. If at that stage it seems insufficiently sweet you can add more sugar and postpone drinking it.

Neutral spirits can also be flavoured with the botanicals used in gin (juniper, citrus peel, cinnamon, angelica, coriander seeds), with dried fruits (prunes, apricots, figs, dates, sultanas, etc.), with herbs, liquorice, celery, with perfumed teas such as Lapsang Souchong and Kusmi Imperial.

The best of the lot is saffron vodka.

No replies/queries/complaints will be attended to in the author's lifetime.

Acknowledgements

I am also indebted in countless different ways to the living, the dead, the fictive.

To all those who have taken a punt on subscribing.

Colette Forder has suffered pluckily for my craft.

BASICS ARE ON PP. 11–23 . . . DON'T WALK AWAY . . . CONCENTRATE . . . FUCK THE GUESTS . . . AND ALL THAT CONVIVIALITY MALARKY . . . DO NOT WASTE BREAD: OIL IT AND REBAKE IT . . . STOCK! GET TREATMENT FOR SQUEAMISHNESS . . . VEGETARIANISM IS CURABLE'

BOOKS REFERRED TO

Charcuterie and French Pork Cookery by Jane Grigson (Penguin, 1975)

Cuisine du Terroir, edited by Céline Vence, translated by Sue Lermon and Simon Mallet (Blenheim House Publishing, 1987)

Cuisine en Famille by Georges Blanc (Albin Michel, 1999)

Cuisine Spontanée by Fredy Girardet, translated by Susan Campbell (Macmillan, 1985)

De Terre et de Mer by Thierry Breton (Robert Laffont, 2004)

Eating Up Italy by Matthew Fort (Fourth Estate, 2004)

English Food by Jane Grigson (Penguin, 1977)

French Provincial Cooking by Elizabeth David (Penguin, 1962)

Goodfellas by Nicholas Pilegi and Martin Scorcese (www.dailyscript.com/scripts/goodfellas.html, 1990)

Inside Mr Enderby by Anthony Burgess (Heinemann, 1963)

Italian Food by Elizabeth David (Penguin, 1954)

Keep It Simple by Alastair Little (Conran Octopus, 1993)

La Cucina Siciliana by Eufemia Azzolina Pupella (Bonechi, 1996)

La Cuisine de la Tupiña by Jean-Pierre Xiradakis (Editions Milan, 2004)

La Cuisinière Provençale by J-B Reboul (Tacussel, 2007)

Le Livre de Cuisine by Jules Gouffé (Librarie Hachette, 1867)

Mastering the Art of French Cooking by Simone Beck, Louisette Bertholle and Julia Child (Penguin, 1968)

Memories of Gascony by Pierre Koffmann (Pyramid, 1990)

My Gastronomy by Nico Ladenis (Macmillan, 1987)

No Place Like Home by Rowley Leigh (Fourth Estate, 2000)

North Atlantic Seafood by Alan Davidson (Penguin, 1980)

Nose to Tail Eating by Fergus Henderson (Macmillan, 1999)

Recettes Paysannnes en Aveyron edited by Philippe Galmiche (Editions Subervie, 1997)

Roast Chicken and Other Stories by Simon Hopkinson and Lindsey Bareham (Ebury Press, 1994)

Spanish Regional Cookery by Ann MacMadhachain (Penguin, 1976)

Testicles: Balls in Cooking and Culture by Blandine Vié, translated by Giles MacDonogh (Prospect Books, 2011)

The Book of Eels by Tom Fort (HarperCollins, 2002)

The Book of Jewish Food by Claudia Roden (Penguin, 1997)

The Cuisine of Paul Bocuse translated by Colette Rossant and Lorraine Davis (Granada, 1985)

The Pedant in the Kitchen by Julian Barnes (Atlantic, 2003)

The Silver Spoon (Phaidon, 2005)

Traité de Cuisine Bourgeoise Bordelaise by Alcide Bontou (Editions Feret, 1898)

You Aren't What You Eat by Steven Poole (Union, 2012)

'SEASON ... SALT ... MAYBE PEPPER (CAN BE WHITE) ... REMOVE THE GERM FROM GARLIC ... COOK SPICES ... BOIL OFF ALCOHOL ... COOK TO PLEASE YOURSELF AS YOU MIGHT WRITE OR PAINT, DANCE OR SING TO PLEASE YOURSELF ... CREATE YOUR OWN THEFTS ...

INDEX

'SEASON ... SALT ... MAYBE PEPPER (CAN BE WHITE) ... REMOVE THE GERM FROM GARLIC ... COOK SPICES ... BOIL OFF ALCOHOL ... COOK TO PLEASE YOURSELF AS YOU MIGHT WRITE OR PAINT, DANCE OR SING TO PLEASE YOURSELF ... CREATE YOUR OWN THEFTS ...

Unbound is the world's first crowdfunding publisher, established in 2011.

We believe that wonderful things can happen when you clear a path for people who share a passion. That's why we've built a platform that brings together readers and authors to crowdfund books they believe in – and give fresh ideas that don't fit the traditional mould the chance they deserve.

This book is in your hands because readers made it possible. Everyone who pledged their support is listed below. Join them by visiting unbound.com and supporting a book today.

Billy Abbott
Anthony Abdool
Alex Aitken
David Aldworth
Mark Alexander
Zena Alkayat
Abigail Allt
Will Alvis
Edward Anderson
Julia Anderson
Nathaniel C R
  Anderson
Igor Andronov
Andy Annett
Phillip Ansell
Scott Anthony
Helen Armfield
Christine Asbury
Lee Ashcroft
Peter Ashley
Michael Atkinson
Steve Ayres

Mark Bailey
Ed Baines
Daniel Baker
Jack Baker
Kieran Baker
Stephen Ball
Jason Ballinger
Ben Barker
Cristian Barnett
Jack Barrie
Robert M W Barton
Kate Bateman
Adam Baylis-West
Jacqui Beazley
Jonathan Beckman
Jaclynne Bell
Linda Bell
David Bennett
Jonathan Bennett
Ignacio Berberana
Terry Bergin
Anne Berkeley

Ben Bessey
Doug Beveridge
Jeremy Blackburn
Michael Blackburn
Alexander Blake
Matthew Blake
Sam Blake
Nathan Bloomfield
David Board
Charlie Bohlen
Tom Borowiecki
Bruce Bowie
Richard Bown
Alan Boyd
Chris Brace
Garret Brady
Louise Brady
Phil Bramley
Doug Branson
Richard W H Bray
Thom Brennan
Tom Brereton

Christian Brett
Neil Brewitt
Matt Frost Bright
John Broadley
Jonathan Brooker
Andrew Brown
Tony Brown
Phil Bruce-Moore
Peter Bullingham
Richard Burgess
Russell Burke
Mike Burn
Johnny Burns
Ian Burrow
Nigel Burwood
Mike Butcher
Tom Byrne
Patrick Campbell
Peter Campbell
James Campen
Xander Cansell
Micah Carr-Hill
Colin Cather
Andrew Catlin
Imogen Challis
Sarah Chamberlain
Jeremy Cherfas
Alexander Chester
Marnie Chesterton
Chris Clarke
Rob Clayton
Jonathan & Rachel
  Clinch
Joe Clinton
Brian Clivaz
Felicity Cloake
Ronnie Clyde
Tom Coady

Simon Cockle
Michael Cohen
Dominic Cole
Philip Connor
Paul G. Convery
Rachel Cooke
Jason Cooper
Jeremy Cooper
Euan Corrall
John Cotcher
Joe Cotter
Joe Coulson
Craig Coulthard
Hugh Counsell
Timothy Cowlishaw
Robert
  Cox-Wrightson
Colin Crawford
John Crawford
Anthony Critchlow
Mick Crossan
Huw Crowley
Paul Cuff
Shannon Cullen
Adam Dant
Rishi Dastidar
Palash Davé
Dan Davies
Maurice Davies
Jon Davison
Steve Day
Henry de Vroome
Celia Deakin
Steve Dempsey
Neil Denny
Magdalena
  Derwojedowa
Morag Deyes

Ciaran Dickinson
Martin Diggins
Les Dodd
Andy Doddington
James Doeser
Miche Doherty
Anne Dolamore
Polona Dolžan
Wendalynn P.
  Donnan
Kevin Donnellon
Paul Duckett
Elizabeth Duff
Andrew Dunn
Christian Dunnage
Rob Dupuis
Daniel Durling
John Durnian
Timothy Dymond
Thom Eagle
Robert Eardley
Brenda Lynn Edgar
Katherine Edward
Cefin Edwards
Michael Eldridge
Dmitry Elentuck
Danielle Ellis
Tony and Christopher
  Elphick
Neil Erskine
Mark Etherton
Nicholas Evans
Duncan Faber
Simon Faircliff
William Falconer
William Farrell
Joshua Feasel
Euan Ferguson

Alex Fiennes
Sally Fincher
Mike Fitzgerald
Robert Fitzgerald
Ben Fletcher-Watson
Tom Flint
Alina Florea
For Peter Lloyd, with
  love
N W Ford
Neil Ford
Bette Forester
Ove Fosså
David Foster
Julian Francis-Lawton
Christine Frazer
Justin Freeman
James Fry
Nocal Gal
Antonia Galloway
Mark Gamble
Alexander Gann
Tom Gardner
Matthew Garrett
Amro Gebreel
Peter Geer
Luke Gilfedder
Neil Gillon
Chris Gittner
Martin Goddard
Tim Godden
George Goodfellow
Giles Goodland
Laura Goodman
Oliver Gorwits
Charlie Gould
Jeremy Gould
Heather Grant

N Grayshon
Fiona Green
Andrew Gregg
Neil Griffiths
Richard Grisdale
Sue Haldemann
Rick Halsall
Susie Harries
Nigel harrison
Lisa Harrod
A.F. Harrold
Peter Hart
Sam Harvey
Guy Haslam
John Hassay
Jonny Haughton
Andrew Hawkins
Jonathan Haynes
Rob Haynes
Elspeth Head
Chris Heathcote
Keith Hector
Simon and Diana
  Heffer
Bea Hemming
Zandy Hemsley
Mark Henderson
Charlie Hicks
Richard Hill
Steve Hill
David G. Hill
  (TurdMinor)
Jonathan Hird
Christopher Hirst
Sandar Hla
Paul Hodges
James Edward
  Hodkinson

George Holland
Kevin Holmes
Leigh Hooper
Scott Horner
Chris Hough
Paul Howard
Ed Howker
Anabel Hudson
Matthew J. Hughes
Cait Hurley
Jim Hutchinson
Laura Washburn
  Hutton
Michael Imber
Phil Inthekitchen
Ian Irvine
Johari Ismail
Roy Isserlis
Daniel Jackson
Martin Jackson
Mark Jefferson
Graham Jeffery
Mark Jeffery
Leonie Jennings
Ric Jerrom
Peter Jewkes
Ellie Johns
Daryl Johnson
Debbie Johnson
Kendra Johnson-
  Matchett
Ian Johnston
David Johnston-Smith
James Johnstone
Tim Rees Jones
Andrew Katz
John Kaye
James Keeping

BASICS ARE ON PP. 11-23 ... DON'T WALK AWAY ... CONCENTRATE ... FUCK THE GUESTS ... AND ALL THAT CONVIVALITY MALARKY ... DO NOT WASTE BREAD: OIL IT AND REBAKE IT ... STOCK! GET TREATMENT FOR SQUEAMISHNESS ... VEGETARIANISM IS CURABLE'

Patric Keller
Anthony Kelly
Martin Kelman
Aidan Kendrick
Jason Kennedy
Ros Kennedy
Rolfe Kentish
Chris Kerridge
Peter Kettle
Jan Kewley
Lucy Key
Malcolm Key
Gregory Khiara
Dan Kieran
Kevin Kieran
George Kinghorn
Doreen Knight
Patrick Knill
Richard Knowles
Adam Koppel
Hanno Koppel
Gregoire Kretz
Dominic Laine
Martin Lam
Nick Lamb
Georgie Laming
Rob Lamond
Tom Lancaster
Ruth Lang
Per Larsson
Dafydd Launder
Craig Lawrie
David Lawson
Paul Lay
Jimmy Leach
Jeremy Lee
Rowley Leigh
Huw Lemmey

Geoff Levett
Paul Levy
Yin Li
Tamasin Little
Bev Littlewood
Paul Lofthouse
Paul Love
Avril Loveless
Pat Lowe
Liz Luck
GJ Lutz
Daniel Lynch
Mike Lynd
Andy Lyons
Sam MacAuslan
Chris Macdonald
Colin MacKenzie
Michelle MacQuarrie
Richard Maggs
Neil Major
Jamie Makin
Elliott Mannis
Kate Manson
Derek Mantle
Pete Marcus
Stephen Markwick
Tom Marshall
Peter Marum-Shaw
Fay Maschler
Sara Masson
Karl Maton
Tracy Matthews (The
    Marmite Museum)
Richard Mayston
Jennifer McConnell
Jonathan McDonagh
Kate McDonnell
NJ McGarrigle

Christian McHugh
Andrew McKie
Bob McLaughlin
Gillian McMullan
JM McVeigh
Fergus McVey
Ian Meikle
Shuna Mercer
Deborah Metters
James Mewis
James Millar
Patrick Miller
Tim Millin
Jon Milloini
Simon Mills
Tracie Misiewicz
Robert Miskin
John Mitchinson
Gordon Moar
Jos Mol
Christopher Daniel
    Moore
Rhiannon Morris
Alan Morton-Smith
Rachel Mosses
Andy Moxon
Andy Muggleton
Philip Murgatroyd
Jane Murison
Damon Murray
Mark Myles
Andrew Nairn
Stu Nathan
Dominic Naughton
Carlo Navato
Brian Newman
Richard Newman
Gary Nicol

'SEASON ... SALT ... MAYBE PEPPER (CAN BE WHITE) ... REMOVE THE GERM FROM GARLIC ... COOK SPICES ... BOIL OFF ALCOHOL ... COOK TO PLEASE YOURSELF AS YOU MIGHT WRITE OR PAINT, DANCE OR SING TO PLEASE YOURSELF ... CREATE YOUR OWN THEFTS ...

Philip Nijman
John Nimmo
Andrew Nixon
Joanna Nixon-
  Proxenos
Jo Norcup
Vaun Earl Norman
Matthew Norwell
Mike O'Brien
Su O'Brien
Alexander O'Broin
Martin O'Callaghan
Sean O'Connell
Eanna O'Lochlainn
John O'Neill
Mark O'Neill
Niall Oakes
Gregory Olver
Emily Oram
David Owen
Mark Owen-Ward
Jenny Owens
Stuart & Lesley
  Oxbrow-Trim
Scott Pack
Sarah Chalmers Page
Michael Paley
Matthew Parden
Nick Parfitt
Michael Parker
Mark Parmenter
Sarah Parnaby
Lulu Parsons
Geoff Patterson
Catherine Payling
Nick Pearson
Ron Pelley
Luke Pendrell

Caroline and James
  Pennock
Blake Perkins
Michael Perrett
Mark Persad
Dan Peters
Sean Peters
Mark Phillips
Catherine Pickersgill
Jonathan Pierpoint
Roger Pietroni
Stephen Pochin
Matthew Poke
Justin Pollard
John Porter
Matthew Porter
Niall Porter
Nicholas Porter
Richard Powell
Anna Powell-Smith
Jean Power
Lisa Pratt
David Preston
Belinda Prince
Jonathan Pugh
Ben Pughe-Morgan
John Pullman
Philip Pullman
Paddy Pulzer
Harry Purser
Deborah Quick
Paul Radford
Glenn Rainey
James Ramsden
Andy Randle
JP Rangaswami
Tom Raw
Jonny Rawlings

James Reader
Nicholas Redding
Alex Renton
Helen Richardson
Nicky Richmond
Mike Rigby
Ewen Roberts
Julian Roberts
Mari Roberts
Graeme Robertson
John Roden
Tony Rogers
Jenny Rollo
Charles Rooney
Tom Roper
Pete Rose
Ian Runacres
Grant Russell
Piers Russell-Cobb
Edward Rustin
Graham Salmon
William Samengo-
  Turner
Tommy Samuel
Jerry Sargent
Martina Angela Sasse
Alex Scott
David Scott
Neil Scott
Patrick Sedgley
Ugur Sendenel
David Sexton
Tracy Sexton
Tony Shannon
Ian Shawyer
Doug Shearer
Tim Sheehy
Samantha Shepherd

BASICS ARE ON PP. 11–23 . . . DON'T WALK AWAY . . . CONCENTRATE . . . FUCK THE GUESTS . . . AND ALL THAT CONVIVALITY MALARKY . . . DO NOT WASTE BREAD: OIL IT AND REBAKE IT . . . STOCK! GET TREATMENT FOR SQUEAMISHNESS . . . VEGETARIANISM IS CURABLE'

Anthony Silverman
Mark Simmons
Marc Skeldon
Paul Skinner
Nigel Slater
Bob Sliman
Meredydd Smart
Gareth L. Smith
Michael Smith
Nigel Smith
Paul Christopher
  Smith
Peter Smith
Theresa Smith
Tasha Snaith
Lili Soh
Joel Somerfield
Stephen Sorrell
Jay Sorrels
Richard Soundy
Andrew Spencer
Owen Stagg
Martina Stansbie
Tom Stapleton
Neil Starr
Richard Stephens
Jason Stewart
Daniel Stilwell
Dominic Stone
Peter Stone
Philip Stout
SubtleBlade
Kirk Surgener
Rory Sutherland
Ben Swales
Christopher Sykes
Sarah T
Karen Tanguy

Christopher Tate
Bryan Taylor
Maisie Taylor
Matthew Taylor
Rob Taylor
Korenne Teeples
George Thain
Nick Timms
James Tobin
Giles Todd
Misti Traya
Jimbaud Turner
Shareef Turner
Ben Tye
Ular Mac Ulsteen
John and Lindsay
  Usher
Stephen Vahrman
Renaud van Strydonck
Mark Vent
Gary Vernon
Emilio Verrecchia
Nicholas Viale
Jose Vizcaino
Bill Wadsworth
Daniel Wainwright
Steve Wake
Francis Walden
George Walden
Richard Walker
Alistair Wallace
Iori Wallace
Dave Walsha
Mark Ward
Jamie Warde-Aldam
Dan Warren
David Warrilow
Nick Watts

Chris Waywell
Oscar Webb
Sam Webb
Andrew Webber
Francis Wheen
Crispin White
Ben Whitehouse
Tim Whitehouse
Seb Whitestone
Miranda Whiting
John Whitworth
Andrew Wiggins
Victoria Wiksen
Simon Wilder
Patrick Wildgust
Will Wiles
Philip Wilkinson
Kendrick Willcocks
Rachel Williams
Sean Williams
Anthony Windram
Sue Winn
Michael Winston
Stephen Wise
Russell Woodward
Jon Woolcott
Adrian and Louise
  Woolrich-Burt
Alex Wright
Phillip Wright
Mike Wynne
Katherine Yelland

'SEASON . . . SALT . . . MAYBE PEPPER (CAN BE WHITE) . . . REMOVE THE GERM FROM GARLIC . . . COOK SPICES . . . BOIL OFF ALCOHOL . . . COOK TO PLEASE YOURSELF AS YOU MIGHT WRITE OR PAINT, DANCE OR SING TO PLEASE YOURSELF . . . CREATE YOUR OWN THEFTS . . .